JOY
EVERY MORNING

JOY
EVERY MORNING

By

MURIEL KOLLER LARSON

MOODY PRESS

CHICAGO

Scripture quotations from *The New International Version,*
copyright © 1978 by The New York International Bible
Society, are used by permission.

Library of Congress Cataloging in Publication Data

Larson, Muriel.
  Joy every morning.
  1. Joy—Meditations. I. Title.
BV4905.2.L27   242   78-23934
ISBN 0-8024-4396-6

Printed in the United States of America

1

Joy Is God's Will for Us

BIBLE READING: Psalm 35:27-28

Rejoice evermore (1 Thessalonians 5:16).

Why have I chosen the theme of joy for this devotional book? Because I am convinced from God's Word that it is His will for every Christian to be joyful.

A widow, whose face glows with love for the Lord and fellow saints, is often lonely, but her joy in the Lord bubbles over and blesses others.

Our pastor has a bounce in his step and a radiant smile for everyone, even though his beautiful redheaded wife has cancer. Countless people have come to Christ through him, and I do not think only his words bore witness; they saw he had something they did not.

Part of it is joy that exhibits itself daily in spite of problems, heartaches, and loneliness. Jesus said that we, His disciples, are the light of the world and should let our lights shine before men. Without His joy, what light would we shed to others?

Your life influences your family, neighbors, co-workers, friends, acquaintances, and people in your church. If you are filled daily with the Lord's joy, you will be a light to all whom you meet and influence them for good and God!

I trust these devotionals will give you daily reasons for rejoicing in the Lord; after 120 days of rejoicing, you will be in the habit!

2

Joy Every Morning

BIBLE READING: Acts 16:22-26

Rejoice in the Lord alway (Philippians 4:4).

While a prisoner in Rome, Paul wrote the Philippians a letter that sounds like a shout of victory. Its theme is joy and rejoicing in the Lord.

Paul knew the secret of victory over anxiety and depression. After telling the Philippians to rejoice in the Lord always, he advised them not to worry about anything, but to bring everything in prayer to the Lord with thanksgiving (Philippians 4:6). Thus, instead of being worried and depressed, the Christian would have God's peace (4:7).

Paul was well acquainted with victory through rejoicing in the Lord. When he and Silas were evangelizing in Philippi, they were arrested, beaten, and imprisoned.

In chains in the rat-infested dungeon, they prayed and sang praises to the Lord. Suddenly an earthquake shook the prison's foundations. The doors flew open; the prisoners were loosed from their shackles.

Similarly, we are loosed from the shackles of depression, anxiety, fears, and worries as we pray and rejoice in the Lord. For how can the flesh keep us down when we are up in the Spirit?

If you rejoiced in the Lord every morning, think what a difference it would make in your life. Practice this when you awaken. Tell the Lord you love Him; then thank and praise Him for every blessing you can think of. Rejoicing in the Lord will soon be a habit.

3

Jesus, Others, You

BIBLE READING: Mark 8:34-38

Whoever finds his life will lose it, and whoever loses his life for my sake will find it (Matthew 10: 39, NIV).

The perfect formula for JOY is *Jesus, Others, You.* It really works! When you put Jesus first in your life, you stay with Him and have the joy He promised His followers (John 15:11). When you are concerned about others and helping and encouraging them, you have no time to wallow in self-pity or self-concern. You see the needs of others, and your heart goes out to them. As you help them spiritually, emotionally, or materially, you will experience a joy unknown to self-centered people.

Sometimes the Lord lays on my heart someone I should phone. Often the person has exclaimed, "Oh, I'm so glad you called! I needed someone to talk to, someone who would pray with me." After talking over their problems and praying, the women often reach a state of serenity and rest in the Lord. I receive the wonderful blessing and joy of knowing I helped.

In Mark 8:34-38, Jesus tells how important it is to never be ashamed of Him. If He is first in our lives, we will want to share His salvation with others.

In Matthew 10:39-42, Jesus says if we give a fellow Christian a cup of cold water because we are His disciples, we will receive a reward.

Where do *You* fit in? With Jesus and others first, *you* will have joy!

4

Tidings of Joy

BIBLE READING: Luke 2:8-14

And my Spirit hath rejoiced in God my Saviour
(Luke 1:47).

As I have interviewed various Christians in order to write
their testimonies, I have been impressed by how many tell of
the peace and joy that filled their hearts when they repented
of their sins and asked Christ to be their Savior.

One woman told me that although she had grown up at-
tending church, she had never found any joy in her religion.
"Sometimes I would come home crying from emptiness,"
Patti said.

Moving to another city, she started attending another
church. The Easter morning service did not particularly stir
her, but three large banners across the front of the church
proclaimed, PEACE, LOVE, JOY.

Well, it's peaceful here, she thought, *and surely in Christianity there must be love. But where is the joy?* Looking at
the faces of those around her, she could see no joy. But oh,
how she yearned for it!

As Patti drove home she passed another church. A sign
with bright blinking lights said: "Revival." Intrigued by
the cheerful display, she went that night and realized that
Christ had died for *her* sins. Yielding her life to Him, her
heart was flooded with joy.

Have you experienced the joy of salvation, the joy of
knowing your sins are forgiven and you are a child of God?
If not, why not receive Christ as your Savior right now?

5

Delight in the Lord

BIBLE READING: Psalm 37:1-9

Delight thyself also in the LORD (v. 4).

For some years I have made it a practice to delight myself in the Lord. How do we delight ourselves in Him? The Hebrew word used in this text for "delight" is 'anag, which means "soft and pliable." One way to freely translate this passage is: "Relax and really enjoy the Lord!"

Consider this good advice by looking at its context and comparing it to the meaning of 'anag. "Trust in the LORD, and do good," the psalmist says. "Commit thy way unto the LORD; trust also in him; and he shall bring it to pass. . . . Rest in the LORD, and wait patiently for him" (vv. 3-7).

A person who lives that way is soft and pliable before the Lord. Delighting herself in the Lord gives her the love and faith to live that way.

If we delight ourselves in the Lord, the promise is: "He shall give thee the desires of thine heart" (v. 4). I can happily testify that the Lord has done that for me. Our main desire when we delight ourselves in the Lord is to know, please, and serve Him. He has helped me do that; He has certainly opened many exciting doors for me to serve Him. In addition, He has blessed me temporally in many ways and has answered many prayers. I say this humbly, as a testimony, because the more He does for and through me, the more I bow before Him in humble awe.

Delight yourself in the Lord, and see what effect it has in your life.

6

Joy in Technicolor

BIBLE READING: Revelation 21:18-24

Trust . . . in the living God, who giveth us richly
all things to enjoy (1 Timothy 6:17).

It is a pity that some people's religion seems to permit
only somber hues! Down through the centuries some professing Christians have clothed themselves in black, as
though they were in mourning for a dead Savior. But Christ
is gloriously alive! Even as He died on the cross, He gave
the victory shout: "It is finished" (John 19:30). Now He
stands at the right hand of God (Acts 7:55). Through His
Spirit He is always present with each Christian (Matthew
28:20).

God splashes magenta, gold, and purple sunsets across
the evening sky. His dawns of gorgeous pink and gold ex-
travaganzas spread across a light blue background. His mul-
tihued rainbows assure us He will never flood the world
again. His dazzling white snow covers the bare winter
ground. His purple, yellow, and red blossoms declare spring.
His gorgeous flowers shout summer. Even fall's dying leaves
reveal His love for beauty.

People, animals, birds, and fish also come in different colors; and their features differ. Would it not be dull if everything looked the same?

God made the grass green and the sky blue, colors which
have a restful effect. Someday we saints shall walk the streets
of gold in a city of pure gold (Revelation 21:18). Yellow
has a cheerful effect, a reminder of how joyful we will be in
the New Jerusalem!

Since God has given us so many colorful things to enjoy,
let us take time to thank God for them.

7
Joy in God's Word
BIBLE READING: Psalm 119:11-18

I rejoice at thy word, as one that findeth great spoil
(Psalm 119:162).

The writing that brings me the greatest joy involves the exposition of God's Word. As I dig into the original Greek or Hebrew words and learn their meanings, joy wells up in my heart so I have to stop what I am doing and rejoice in the Lord and His Word.

I often experience this joy when I am reading God's Word devotionally and a passage strikes me with new meaning. How exciting God's Word is when we come to it expectantly, looking for Him to speak to our hearts through it.

Psalm 119 exults in God's Word: His testimonies, commandments, statutes, precepts, Law, judgments, ordinances. Yet the men who wrote this psalm did not have the New Testament with its wisdom and its accounts of God's sojourn on earth. We do. In the New Testament is something more marvelous than Law: the grace of God that reveals His love for us.

When my husband was going to Bible college, I memorized two Bible verses daily as I walked to work, also repeating those I already had learned. Never were the colors and fragrance of God's flowers more beautiful, or the sound of His creatures more sweet. God's Word was the cause. His Word is not only beautiful; it makes everything else beautiful, too — including us.

As you read God's Word in the days to come, ask Him to open your eyes to its beauty and truth. Then see how the joy will bubble up in your soul, too.

8

Joy Unspeakable

BIBLE READING: 1 Peter 1:3-8

Rejoice with joy unspeakable and full of glory
(v. 8).

The church was about thirty-five years old when Peter
wrote his first letter to the Christians in Asia Minor. Shortly
thereafter, Nero would commence his terrible persecution of
Christians.

It was literally a "fiery trial." Christians in Rome were
burned nightly to light up Nero's gardens. And Nero is
said to have ordered the city set on fire and then blamed the
Christians. Throughout Rome, Christians were arrested and
thrown into prison, and some died for their faith. So those
to whom Peter wrote were "in heaviness through manifold
temptations" (v. 6).

However, Peter comforted them by saying that the trial
of their faith, which was more precious than gold, would
bring them much praise, honor, and glory when Christ returned to earth. Apparently, however, he knew they were
not letting their trials get them down, for he said plainly
that they were rejoicing in Christ with joy unspeakable and
full of glory!

Compare your problems with those of these saints. Have
any of your loved ones been burned at a stake? Do you lie
in chains in a dank prison, your back torn to ribbons, and
rats scampering close by? Do you worship with one eye
on the door, expecting soldiers to burst in at any minute and
take you to jail, torture, death — or worse? Christians in
some Communist lands live like this.

Rejoice in Jesus with joy unspeakable and full of glory!

9

Joy in God's Mercies

BIBLE READING: Psalm 103:1-17

I will sing of the mercies of the LORD for ever (Psalm 89:1).

Whenever I see the phrase "Bless the Lord," I think of joy. When we bless the Lord, we get the blessing, especially in the return of joy.

What is the greatest way in which God has shown His mercy toward us? He "forgiveth all thine iniquities" (Psalm 103:3) and saves our souls. In spite of the many ways in which we offend Him, He often spares our lives.

A young man, who was a Hell's Angel for seven years, had taken all kinds of drugs, eventually becoming a Satan worshiper. Rick's drug habit cost him fifty dollars a day, which he had to steal. In despair he took an overdose of heroin and crawled into a garbage can to die. But God in His mercy kept Rick alive; then He brought him to Christ. Now Rick is in the Lord's service.

Our personal salvation story may not be as dramatic; nonetheless, the Lord had mercy on us in spite of our innate sinfulness. He has shown mercy many times in being patient with us even after we became Christians. He pities, comforts, and helps us in all trials.

"The LORD is good to all: and his tender mercies are over all his works" (Psalm 145:9). Jesus said not one sparrow falls to the ground without our Father's knowing, and that we are of more value than many sparrows (Matthew 10:29-31).

Think of God's mercies toward you, and bless Him for them; then experience His joy.

10

Rejoice with Trembling

BIBLE READING: Psalm 2

Serve the LORD with fear, and rejoice with trembling (v. 11).

God wants us to have joy, but joy in what? To the majority of people, joy is derived from earthly pleasures—partying, a bottle, lovemaking, work, or play. Earthly joy may not necessarily be sinful, but it could detract from rejoicing in the Lord.

The psalmist says a strange thing here: "Rejoice with trembling." Matthew Henry says this means we should rejoice "with a holy awe of him, a holy fear for ourselves, lest we come short, and a tender concern for the many precious souls to whom his gospel and kingdom are a savour of death unto death. Whatever we rejoice in, in this world, it must always be with trembling, lest we grow vain in our joy and be puffed up with the things we rejoice in."

"Rejoice with trembling" goes with serving and worshiping the Lord with reverence. Are we conscious of the awesome responsibility we have as His servants to do His will and to reach a dying world for Him? Are we so thrilled with the work He has entrusted to us that we rejoice in Him day and night?

"Kiss the Son," the psalmist also advises (v. 12). What woman can know anything about real rejoicing until she receives the Savior and accepts Him into her life? No joy is like that of knowing Him and abiding in Him! Let Him be precious to you, love Him with all your heart, wet His feet with your kisses and tears. He is altogether lovely. Rejoice in Jesus!

11

Joy of the Lowly

BIBLE READING: Matthew 5:1-12

> Blessed are the poor in spirit: for theirs is the kingdom of heaven (v. 3).

The Greek word *makarios,* used in the Beatitudes of Jesus may be translated either as "blessed" or "happy." Assuredly, the Christian who has the Lord's kind of happiness will have joy!

But Psalm 51:17 says, "The sacrifices of God are a broken spirit: a broken and a contrite heart, O God, thou wilt not despise." How on earth can a person be happy if her spirit is broken? The Bible is full of paradoxes, such as this. A woman has to come to an end of herself, of depending on her own works, in order to cast herself on Christ and depend on Him alone for salvation.

Mary, a member of a Bible-believing church for years, prided herself on her good life. When the Holy Spirit convicted her of being lost, she reminded God, "But You know I'm good, Lord. I have lived a good life. I've never smoked, drunk, gone to movies or public swimming beaches, danced, or worn makeup. I've tithed. I've served You all these years, and I've led people to Christ!"

But as Mary continued to be convicted, she remembered that although she had gone forward in church, she had never repented of sin or realized Christ had died for her. Mary finally came to an end of herself and gave her heart to Christ.

The day that she yielded to the Lord, Mary became poor in spirit. In awe, she felt humble and unworthy at the thought that the Son of God would actually die for her!

12

Joy of the Humble

BIBLE READING: 1 Peter 5:3-6

Blessed are the meek: for they shall inherit the earth (Matthew 5:5).

Savor the beautiful expanded translation of Matthew 5:5 in the *Amplified Bible:* "Blessed—happy, blithesome, joyous, spiritually prosperous [that is, with life-joy and satisfaction in God's favor and salvation, regardless of their outward conditions]—are the meek (the mild, patient, long-suffering), for they shall inherit the earth!"

The above description of "blessed," found between the dashes, can be used for a richer understanding of the Beatitudes. But Jesus says that she who is humble, patient, and long-suffering is happy and will have life-joy and satisfaction in God's favor and salvation, regardless of outward conditions.

What gets in the way of being humble, patient, and long-suffering? Our pride. *I* do not like to be put down. *I* do not like to be kept waiting. *I* do not like people mistreating, humiliating, and snubbing *me.* Why did they not give *me* that position? Why does God not answer *my* prayer immediately? Why do *I* have to continue to bear this [illness, burden, husband, child, neighbor]? (Take your choice!)

If we are God's children, is He not in perfect control of our lives? He will work all things together for good. He knows what is best, and He can take the rough places in our lives and use them for His glory and our eternal reward. True humility results from trusting God and putting His glory above our gain. Then we will have life-joy and satisfaction in God.

13

Joy of the Spiritually Hungry

BIBLE READING: Psalm 84

Blessed are they which do hunger and thirst after righteousness: for they shall be filled (Matthew 5:6).

When I was twenty-four, I lived to please myself. At my card club I drank and gambled until dawn. I also played the piano with my brother's dance band. God had little place in my thoughts.

My husband decided to go to business school, so we put our little girl in a day nursery and I got a job. God sent a missionary candidate to work with me and to live Christ before me. Comparing her pure, dedicated life with my frivolous, self-centered one, I became convicted. I saw Lillian had something I did not have, and I began yearning for it.

One day a janitor left a gospel tract on my desk. When I read it, I realized that Christ died for *my* sins. Weeping, I bowed my head and gave myself to Him.

As I continued to hunger and thirst after righteousness, I grew spiritually. I had the joy of seeing every member of my family come to know Christ, too.

The Greek word for "filled" in Matthew 5:6 is *chortazo,* which means "completely satisfied." I experienced the joy of becoming completely satisfied as I learned that Christ's righteousness was imputed to me and that the Holy Spirit was working in me to conform me to Christ's image (Romans 8:29; Philippians 1:6). These beautiful truths are for you, too. What joy we can experience as God gives us the victory over bad habits and makes us right with Him.

14

Joy of the Merciful

BIBLE READING: Luke 6:35-38

Blessed are the merciful: for they shall obtain mercy (Matthew 5:7).

What is mercy? The Greek word used for mercy in the above Scripture is *eleeo;* it means to have compassion by word or deed. Mercy is affectionate pity for those who are needy, distressed, or suffering in any way. It fosters a forgiving spirit toward all men.

We Christians are the objects of God's mercy. God pitied us (Psalm 103:13); loved us even while we were yet sinners (Romans 5:8); forgave us (Ephesians 4:32); and saved us (Romans 10:13). We are His children and must be merciful as He is.

Hannah Hurnard, British missionary to Jews and Arabs in Palestine, spent five years going through the land to tell every village of Christ. She and her co-workers traveled thousands of miles over rough roads, suffering abuse and living under primitive conditions. But though they denied themselves because of their compassion for those who had never heard of Christ, they had great joy in being the first to take the Good News to many. Miss Hurnard wrote, "How full of unspeakable joy and blessing, along with conflict, those five years had been!"

Taking the gospel to the lost is one way of being merciful. Doing deeds of kindness is another. Visiting the sick, shut-ins, prisoners: that is mercy. Being ready to overlook and forgive: that is mercy. Encouraging the outcasts, the down-hearted, the discouraged, the backsliders: that is mercy.

When we are merciful toward others, we are happy; we have the joy of the Lord!

15

Joy of the Peacemaker

BIBLE READING: James 3:6-18

> Blessed are the peacemakers: for they shall be called the children of God (Matthew 5:9).

Do we have more peacemakers or troublemakers in this world today? How about in our churches? Troublemakers stand out. Everyone from the pastor on down gets blistered by the tongues set on fire by hell (James 3:6).

Troublemaking is satanic, for the devil is the "accuser of our brethren" (Revelation 12:10). No wonder so many Christians lack the joy of the Lord, for we unwittingly join Satan in his unholy work as a troublemaker. We hurt the cause of Christ by gossiping about or criticizing our fellow Christians.

On the other hand, we can easily find all sorts of opportunities to bring peace in our churches, homes, and neighborhoods. One Sunday morning I saw a distressed look on a friend's face. After the service I asked her how things were. "Pretty bad," Charlene replied grimly. "Ellen and I have had a big misunderstanding, and now she won't even speak to me!"

"Well, look," I said, "even if you feel you've done nothing wrong, why don't you call or write Ellen and apologize if you've offended her in any way, and ask her for a chance to talk things over?"

Charlene agreed. That night at the evening service she looked her usual cheerful self. Afterward she told me she had called Ellen and apologized. They had talked things out, and everything was fine.

That moment I knew exactly what Matthew 5:9 meant. Look for ways to be a peacemaker.

16

Joy of the Repentant

BIBLE READING: Acts 3:14-19

Blessed are they that mourn: for they shall be comforted (Matthew 5:4).

Here is another paradox! How can you be happy when you mourn? Jesus gave part of the answer when He promised that those who mourn shall be comforted.

What are we supposed to mourn about? Our sins, things in our lives that displease God, our lukewarmness, lack of devotion, self-centeredness, failure to serve Him—whatever the Holy Spirit convicts us about (John 16:7-11).

Those who mourn over their lost condition when the Holy Spirit convicts them will repent, give their hearts to Christ, and know true joy.

Christians who are sensitive to the voice of the Holy Spirit grieve when they do something wrong. They soon confess their sin and get right with God, thus having their joy restored. Those who truly mourn over a wrongdoing will certainly think twice before doing that thing again! True repentance includes turning from wrongdoing.

Helen told me how she had fallen away from the Lord, stopped attending church regularly, and had quit reading her Bible and trying to live for the Lord. For several years she had no real peace or joy.

Finally God spoke to Helen through the death of her sister, who accepted Christ as her Savior just before she died. When Helen mourned her backsliding and returned to the Lord, His joy once again filled her heart.

17

Joy of the Pure in Heart

BIBLE READING: Psalm 24

> Blessed are the pure in heart: for they shall see God (Matthew 5:8).

True Christianity stems from the heart. When we ask Christ to come into our hearts, He comes in and gives us *new* hearts (Ezekiel 18:31). This makes us new persons (2 Corinthians 5:17) with new desires, especially the desire to live for the Lord and please Him. Our sins are washed away, and we become pure in heart. Love bubbles out of this pure heart toward God and our fellowmen.

When we are first saved and have that beautifully pure and single heart, we have joy. Why do we lose that joy? Because we allow sin to muddy the purity of our hearts. We Christians have what might be termed a "split personality." We have that new heart from the Lord, but we still have the old fleshy nature that keeps trying to assert itself (see Romans 7). Jesus said, "For from within, out of men's hearts, come evil thoughts" (Mark 7:21, NIV).

The Greek word used for "heart" in Mark 7:21 is *kardia,* which means the heart, thoughts, feelings, or mind. Out of our fleshly minds arise thoughts and impulses of the "old man" that may influence our actions. The Bible tells us, "Put off your old self, which is being corrupted by its deceitful desires; to be made new in the attitude of your minds; and to put on the new self, created to be like God in true righteousness and holiness" (Ephesians 4:22-24, NIV).

First John 1:9 says, "If we confess our sins, he is faithful and just to forgive us our sins, and to cleanse us from all unrighteousness." If we do this regularly, we will have joy.

18

Joy of the Persecuted

BIBLE READING: 1 Peter 4:12-16

Blessed are they which are persecuted for righteousness' sake: for theirs is the kingdom of
heaven. Blessed are ye, when men shall revile you,
and persecute you, and shall say all manner of evil
against you falsely, for my sake (Matthew 5:10-
11).

In the early days of the church, Christians were often
severely persecuted. *Foxe's Book of Martyrs* says, however,
that the inscriptions on their tombs in the catacombs beneath Rome "breathe forth peace and joy and triumph."

Foxe told of two Christian sisters who lived during the
persecution under the Roman emperor Valerian. Rufina
and Secunda were engaged to two noblemen, also professing
Christians. As the persecution increased and threatened
their fortunes, the men renounced their faith; but the sisters
stood firm. Angered, the two men betrayed them; the girls
were apprehended and sealed their testimonies with their
blood.

If you are standing for Christ you may be undergoing persecution. Peter wrote: "Beloved, think it not strange concerning the fiery trial which is to try you . . . but rejoice,
inasmuch as ye are partakers of Christ's sufferings" (1 Peter
4:12-13).

When your husband hits you because you have been to
church—when your neighbor puts tacks in your driveway
so you will get flat tires (as I did!)—when a professing
Christian maligns you because of your stand for Christ,
Jesus says, "Rejoice, and be exceeding glad" (Matthew 5:
12).

22

19

Stop—and Praise the Lord!

BIBLE READING: Psalm 100

Let every thing that hath breath praise the LORD (Psalm 150:6).

One morning as I bustled about the house trying to get some things done, I heard the clear, sweet song of a mockingbird piped in through the fireplace in my living room. I paused and listened. Then I sat down cross-legged by the fireplace just to enjoy that gray-and-white songbird perched on my chimney.

What a restful experience! As I sat there, I wondered, *Why does that mockingbird sing so much? Is he praising his Creator with his singing?* So I started praising and thanking my Lord for all His blessings.

As I arose to resume my work a few minutes later, I had new vigor for my tasks and my heart bubbled over with joy.

Sometimes I think we get so busy in our everyday life that we forget to praise and thank the Lord. Could this be why our work becomes a burden at times? Could this be why we lose our joy in the Lord? The Bible says "Bless the LORD, O my soul, and forget not all his benefits" (Psalm 103:2).

Every morning when I awake I praise the Lord and thank Him for various blessings. This really gets my day off to a good, cheerful start! One blessing I often praise the Lord for is my unearned salvation. This reminds me how much my heavenly Father and my Savior love me, and it fills me with joy. "If God be for us, who can be against us?" (Romans 8:31).

20

Joy in God's Protection

BIBLE READING: Psalm 91:1-11

He is my refuge and my fortress (v. 2).

Have you ever had a narrow escape and realized that the Lord must have surely been protecting you? After several close ones while driving, I have been thrilled and full of thanksgiving to God for His protection.

We all know how God sent an angel to protect Shadrach, Meshach, and Abednego in the fiery furnace. We know how He sent an angel to shut the lions' mouths so that they could not eat Daniel (Daniel 6:22). We know how an angel delivered Peter from prison and certain death. But do we realize that we are just as precious to God as those saints were—and that God changes not?

When Corrie ten Boom was carrying Russian Bibles in her suitcase for Christians in the USSR, a Moscow customs officer ransacked the suitcase of the person ahead of her. Corrie prayed. When she raised her head, she saw beings of light—angels—surrounding her suitcase. Then they vanished. The customs officer picked up her suitcase—remarked on how heavy it was—and then carried it to her car for her!

On the other hand, the Lord had allowed Corrie and her sister Betsie to be put into a horrible concentration camp, where He used them as His witnesses. Although the Lord took the weakened Betsie home to glory, He miraculously saved Corrie from the gas chambers through a clerical error. A week later, she was released.

21

Joy in God's Omnipotence

BIBLE READING: Psalm 145

Is anything too hard for the LORD? (Genesis 18:
14).

Why do we tend to limit God, even though we are familiar with His mighty works? Even the blessed Mary, chosen vessel of God, could not understand how she could be the mother of a child without knowing a man. An angel told her the Holy Spirit would come upon her and His power would overshadow her.

"For that reason the holy offspring shall be called the Son of God" (Luke 1:35*b*, NASB), the angel explained. Then he told Mary how her cousin, Elizabeth, who was past the age of childbearing, was also going to have a son. He concluded by saying, "For with God nothing shall be impossible" (Luke 1:37). Do you believe that with all your heart? Read Psalm 145, letting its blessed truths sink into your heart and mind. Think about them, savor them, and then follow the psalmist's example of praise.

I love the book of Ephesians. Listen to this: "Now unto him that is able to do exceeding abundantly above all that we ask or think, according to the power that worketh in us, unto him be glory" (3:20-21). Does it not fill your heart with faith when you realize how all-powerful our Lord is?

Paul, inspired of God, said to the Ephesian believers:

I pray also that the eyes of your heart may be enlightened in order that you may know the hope to which he has called you, the riches of his glorious inheritance in the saints, and his incomparably great power for us who believe (1:18-19, NIV).

22

Joy in God's Omnipresence

BIBLE READING: Psalm 139:1-10

Am I a God at hand? (Jeremiah 23:23).

Here is an atheist named George, lying with a mysterious illness in a hospital bed, pondering what his roommate has told him about Jesus Christ. At two o'clock in the morning he slips out of bed and falls on his knees. *O God,* he cries silently, *forgive me my sins. I believe that Jesus died for me!* Peace such as he has never known before floods his soul. God is there.

Here is a fifteen-year-old girl named Debbie, whose difficult life and atheistic relatives have made her an agnostic. But her heart cries out, *If You really are, God, show me. If You will give me a white cat, I'll believe in You.* Shortly after that, while she is riding home on her bicycle, she sees a bedraggled white cat in the middle of the road. The cat turns out to be a beautiful Persian, and no one claims it. "I believe in You now, God!" exclaims Debbie. God is there.

Here is Muriel, driving down a superhighway in Texas at top speed. Her husband takes their baby daughter into his arms. A moment later Muriel sees a car pull out of a service road and stop, straddling the highway. She slams on the brakes and stops two feet from the car. If her husband had not picked up the baby moments before, she might have been killed. God is there.

Praise the Lord! God is everywhere!

23

Joy in God's Omniscience

BIBLE READING: Matthew 6:1-8

Thou God seest me (Genesis 16:13).

When my husband pastored a Wisconsin church, a lady left food gifts in our car every prayer meeting night. They would be either a dozen eggs and a loaf of homemade bread, or cake, or cookies, or a bag of tomatoes. At first we did not know who left them. Then we realized who it was as we ate in her home. But God knew, and I am sure that someday He will reward her openly.

God knows everything. He sees everything we do. He knows about the little kind deeds you do for others. He knows the ways in which you serve your church, for which you receive no reward in this life. Let others receive pay or glory here. Your reward in heaven will be far more glorious!

God knows our hearts. He knows how sorry we are when we slip and fail Him. He knows our yearning to please Him. He understands our frailties, for He became a man Himself (Hebrews 4:15).

God knows our needs (Matthew 6:8). Isobel Kuhn, in *Green Leaf in Drought Time,* told of Wilda and Arthur Mathews, missionaries in China when the Communists took over. Often it seemed as if they would not have food, but God supplied their needs day by day. He will meet *all* our needs if we will look to Him (Philippians 4:19).

What is your need today? God knows what it is, but talk to Him about it, for He loves to have you bring your needs to Him, in a simple, trusting way.

24

Joy in Our Children

BIBLE READING: Psalm 127

Behold, children are a gift of the LORD (v. 3, NASB).

I can just hear some mothers saying, "What? Children a joy? Mine are driving me straight up the wall!" But I can hear others saying, "Oh, how sweet it is to me to have their little arms wrapped around my neck and hear them say, 'I love you, Mommy.'"

There are both frustrations and joys in rearing children. One of your children may have a sweet disposition and be tractable, while another may be as difficult as all get out. It is hard to explain. On the other hand, the tractable one may not be affectionate but the little rascal may make you feel you are the best mommy in the world!

The Lord has given us these precious ones to rear for Him. Each individual personality needs an individual touch, although all need a lot of love and discipline. We need to seek the Lord's wisdom in order to develop properly those souls, those characters, that are entrusted to us by Him!

As mothers we can derive great joy from this fact: molding a life for the glory of God is more important than being a business success, writing a book, attaining stardom, or even being President of the United States. If your child is reared to serve the Lord, who knows how many others will get to heaven because of the good job you have done with the one given into your hand?

Think of your children and rejoice in the way the Lord is going to help you to rear servants of God!

25

Joy in God's Justice

BIBLE READING: Romans 12:17-21

Vengeance is mine; I will repay, saith the Lord
(v. 19).

God is love and plenteous in mercy, and He gives eternal
life to those who trust in Christ. But judgment awaits those
who are outside Christ. And God has instituted a system
whereby people pay for their foolishness and meanness.

The Lord assures us that justice will be done, that He will
avenge evil. This makes it possible for us to obey Him and
be charitable toward those who wrong us. "Overcome evil
with good," God tells us (v. 21).

A neighbor sprayed the honeysuckle vine on my fence
with poison, killing it. It made me angry, but I took it to
God, who pacified me and put charity in my heart toward
the woman. Eventually we became the best of friends.
What she did could have caused constant enmity; then
where would my joy have been?

Bernice's husband frequently cursed and berated her. She
got even by not speaking to him for days. When she did
speak, it was in as nasty a tone as he had used. And she
found various ways in which to belittle him. Needless to
say, she did not know what peace was—or joy, either! If she
had asked the Lord to help her return good for evil, she
might have been able to reduce the contention in her home.

Has anyone been giving you a hard time? Commit that
one to the Lord. Let Him take care of the justice. Just love
that one who has despitefully used you, and pray for him,
as Jesus said. Hatred and bitterness cause misery, but a
charitable spirit results in joy.

26

Joy in the Lord

BIBLE READING: Psalm 147:1-7

Thou shalt rejoice in the LORD, and shalt glory in
the Holy One of Israel (Isaiah 41:16).

So often we Christians tend to take our Lord for granted.
Do we ever stop and think of Him as a person? Do we ever
rejoice in Him as David did?

God called David "a man after mine own heart" (Acts
13:22), and I think the reason He called him that is
found in the book of Psalms. If we would like God to call
us, "women after mine own heart," then let us learn by reading the Psalms over and over how David rejoiced in God!

In Psalm 34:2-3 the joy David found in God is plain. He
sang, "My soul shall make her boast in the LORD: the humble shall hear thereof, and be glad. O magnify the LORD with
me, and let us exalt his name together."

The apostle Paul wrote, "He that glorieth, let him glory
in the Lord" (1 Corinthians 1:31). How much time do we
Christians spend just thinking of our wonderful Lord, just
rejoicing in Him? How would it affect our lives if we de-
voted ten or fifteen minutes a day to seeking our joy in God?
I think it would do far more good than tranquilizers!

I know one woman who seeks her pacifier from whiskey.
What a mess she is making of her life! Another says she
just has to have cigarettes to keep her calm. Others need
their uppers or downers. All a Christian woman needs to get
a "high" for the day is to seek her joy in the Lord.

27

Joy in God's Blessings

BIBLE READING: Matthew 6:24-34

But my God shall supply all your need according to his riches in glory by Christ Jesus (Philippians 4:19).

Perhaps the reason many Christians are not filled with the Lord's joy is that they accept God's blessings day after day without thanking Him.

Just think about your body and health, for instance. Are you grateful for a good digestive system? Or if you do not have such a good one, do you thank God for those parts of your body that do work well?

I have a tendency toward chronic bronchitis that has an unpleasant habit of popping up sometimes when I have a speaking engagement or must sing a solo at church. But I am truly thankful to the Lord that I can get around on my own, that I have plenty of energy, and that I can see, hear, and think. Why dwell on things that are wrong when we are blessed by the Lord with so many other things?

I am even thankful for my bronchitis, because it keeps me dependent upon God; I know I do a far better job as His servant than if I were completely self-sufficient. The bronchitis flared up once when I was to appear on television, and another time when I was on a radio interview program. In both cases, the Lord kept me from coughing.

God may not give us everything we want, but He supplies all our needs (Philippians 4:19). Paul, who went hungry at times, said that. Through his rough experiences, he learned to be content. From prison he wrote, "Rejoice in the Lord always!" (Philippians 4:4, NIV).

31

28

Joy of Deliverance from Depression

BIBLE READING: Psalm 28

For thou hast lifted me up (Psalm 30:1).

Two days before I was to go to teach at a Christian writers' conference, I was hit by two stunning blows. One was a family matter, and the other was a keen disappointment in my writing work. Something fell through that I had ardently yearned to do. Ordinarily, rejections from publishers bother me very little (I accept them as from the Lord), but this one really hurt!

The twin blows sent me reeling down to the depths of depression, a place I very seldom go. I walked around the house in a gloomy trance, doing what had to be done and having no ambition to write.

But then I started thinking about the writers' conference, where I wanted to be a blessing and inspiration. How could I be if I was not filled with the joy of the Lord? I knew how to get that joy back. I had to start thanking and praising the Lord for something about those disappointments.

Regarding the family matter, I found I could praise and thank Him because the problem had been discovered in time. Concerning the writing disappointment, I started thanking the Lord that His hand was on all of my writing; it was His work, not mine. If He had closed that door, then He had something better in mind.

As I praised and thanked the Lord, His joy flooded my heart! And at the conference, He gave me numerous opportunities to help and encourage fellow writers spiritually. I had joy running over, enough to share with others!

29

Joy in Deliverance from Fear

BIBLE READING: Psalm 34:1-8

I sought the LORD, and he heard me, and delivered
me from all my fears (Psalm 34:4).

Does a recurrent fear trouble you and rob you of peace
and joy? Marital troubles, financial problems, illness, or
psychological hang-ups might fill your heart with fear.

But if you have Christ in your heart, you are a special
person! You are God's own child, an heir with Christ, and
"God hath not given us the spirit of fear; but of power, and
of love and of a sound mind" (2 Timothy 1:7). Why then
do Christians sometimes suffer from the worry and anxiety
that fear causes?

When my daughter Lori was seven, she suffered from
imaginary fears. One day while praying for her, I realized
that the opposite of fear was faith. *Perhaps her decision for
Christ was only in her head,* I thought. So I prayed that if
this were so, she would truly come to know Christ as
Savior.

One month later Lori came under deep conviction of sin
and her need to be saved. I once again helped her pray to
receive Christ as her Savior. That night she was gloriously
delivered from all her fears.

Later, when her faith was no longer new, a little fear came
back. And that is how it is with us if we do not stay close
to our Savior day by day—doing His will, reading His Word,
and spending time with Him.

He is always able to deliver us from all our fears and
give us joy.

30

Joy in God's Immutability

BIBLE READING: James 1:17-22

I am the LORD, I change not (Malachi 3:6).

If a human being promises us something, he may keep his promise, or for some reason he may break it, willingly or unwillingly. Man is changeable; God is not. Man is limited in what he can do; God is not.

Many professing Christians today claim that the moral standard for Christians has changed. They say that what a Christian does depends upon the situation; as long as love is involved, or a meaningful relationship, whatever he does is OK.

Not so! God is unchangeable; what was an abomination to Him four thousand years ago is still an abomination to-day. For instance, witchcraft—white or black (Deuteronomy 18:10-12) and homosexuality, as well as all kinds of immorality (Jeremiah 23:14) are abominations to God.

Sin is still sin as set forth in God's Word. But the blind lead the blind, and they all fall into the ditches: of gruesome diseases that waste the body and mind; of abortions and indiscretions and haunting guilt; of the consequences of following man's philosophies instead of God's will.

We who love the Lord need not wander in the darkness of theory or wonder about how we might enjoy the best kind of life. God's Word is still applicable today. It gives us a sure guide to peace, joy, and abundant life. It warns of the pitfalls of sin and of the fallacies of man's wisdom, and it shares the teachings of Christ, who is "the same yesterday, and to day, and for ever" (Hebrews 13:8). Rejoice in our dependable Lord!

31

Joy in God's Wisdom

BIBLE READING: Proverbs 3:13-24

He giveth wisdom unto the wise (Daniel 2:21).

Sometimes we may be tempted to question God: "Why did You do this, Lord?" Anger, which robs us of joy, may arise in our hearts against the all-wise God. But how much do we know about the future? Do we know all the details about any given situation or person? Are we as wise and omniscient as God? "The foolishness of God is wiser than men" (1 Corinthians 1:25).

I knew a family that was far from God. They had five children, and the sweetest one was the youngest girl, a three-year-old with blond, curly hair. One day she wandered into the path of a trolley and was instantly killed. Everyone was horrified, including myself. Why had this innocent girl been killed?

I did not understand until years later, when I read in 1 Kings 14 how King Jeroboam's son fell ill. The prophet Ahijah told Jeroboam's wife God was going to judge Jeroboam's house, but the boy would die before that happened, "because in him there is found some good thing" (v. 13). God took the boy to paradise rather than let him grow up and become polluted by his family and suffer its fate. Dying is graduation time for those who love the Lord!

If we trust implicitly in the Lord's wisdom, we will always rejoice. If we ask God in faith for wisdom, He will share it with us (James 1:5). If we handled our problems with God's wisdom, we would save ourselves and our loved ones a lot of grief. It is hard to have joy when we are miserable!

32

Making Melody

BIBLE READING: Colossians 3:12-17

Singing and making melody in your heart to the Lord (Ephesians 5:19).

"Her voice is set to music, a miracle to the people here who know only how to groan and grumble. She is ever praising the Lord and her testimony to the Saviour is not a shabby one."

This eulogy was written about a Christian woman. A well-fed, well-dressed, comfortable-living woman in America? No, this was a blind Black woman who lived in Africa, and about whom Mary Slessor, the well-known "white queen of the cannibals," wrote. She also said about blind Mary:

> She is so poor that she has not one farthing in this world but what she gets from us, not a creature to do a thing for her, her house all open to rain and ruin, and into which the cows rush at times. But blind Mary is our living, bright, clear light.

Just think of her life! Yet her voice was "set to music" amid a land of grumblers and complainers. What a contrast she must have been to those around her. What a contrast to those of us who live so comfortably!

How would our daily outlook on life be affected if we were always praising the Lord instead of complaining? It is easy to get into the habit of grumbling, but it makes us and those who have to live with us miserable. It surely does not glorify the Lord or reveal Christ in us! And we rob ourselves of so much joy that our Lord wants us to have.

Sing and make melody in your heart every day, and that joy will be yours.

33

Joy in God's Sovereignty

BIBLE READING: 1 Samuel 2:1-10

My times are in thy hand (Psalm 31:15).

One of the most beautiful, Spirit-inspired psalms of joy in God's sovereignty was sung by a woman, Hannah. How she rejoiced when her prayer for a son was answered! I know how she must have felt. I had one daughter, and then I prayed for thirteen years for another child. Then God gave me Lori.

Again and again since that thrilling day when Lori was born, I have realized that God's timing was just right. On many other occasions I have been aware that my times are in His omnipotent hand. So I have learned to trust His timing instead of my own, to rest in His sovereignty.

God is in charge. We Christians do not have to worry and fret, as the lost do, about what is going to happen on earth. The heathen may rage, but God shall laugh at them (Psalm 2:1-4). Someday His Son shall rule the world.

Inflation and unemployment may run rampant, but God will supply all our needs. Wars and rumors of wars, earthquakes and hurricanes, famines and pestilences may come, but our times are in God's hands. Nothing can separate us from His love (Romans 8:38-39). Nothing can touch us unless it comes through His hand of love, in which we Christians rest (John 10:28).

So rejoice in God's sovereignty, sister in Christ. Praise and thank Him that He is over all and in all. With the great multitude of Revelation 19:6 say, "Alleluia: for the Lord God omnipotent reigneth."

34

Lasting Joy

BIBLE READING: Psalm 16:5-11

In thy presence is fulness of joy; at thy right hand
there are pleasures for evermore (v. 11).

A well-known psychiatrist said, "Happy people have
better health. They stand out in a crowd. They seem to
grow old slowly. They have good muscle tone, skin color
and coordination. Their eyes are bright, their posture erect,
and their digestion is good."

The surest way to fit this description is to walk daily with
the Lord. To walk with Him, we must repent of our sins
and receive Christ as Savior. To keep walking with Him,
we have to give Him control of our hearts, actions, and
thoughts.

In spite of numerous trials and persecutions, the apostle
Paul must have been happy. He used the words *rejoice* and
joy many times in his epistles. He was happy because he
walked close to the Lord daily.

Paul wrote, "We are troubled on every side, yet not distressed; we are perplexed, but not in despair; persecuted,
but not forsaken; cast down, but not destroyed" (2 Corinthians 4:8-9). You may have pain, problems, temptations,
and trials; but if you are abiding in Christ, "the joy of the
LORD is your strength" (Nehemiah 8:10), just as it was
Paul's.

Living for and with Jesus, we can have joy forevermore,
starting now. He will guide us in the paths of right living
and give us wisdom for the care of our bodies.

35

Joy in Righteousness

BIBLE READING: Psalm 68

The righteous doth sing and rejoice (Proverbs 29:
6).

Who are the righteous? God's people, who have been
washed by the blood of Christ (1 Peter 1:18-19) and now
live for the Lord.

I do not know why some people think that all they have
to do to obtain eternal life is to go forward in church and
make a superficial profession of faith in Christ—and then
live as they please! If anyone is truly in Christ, she becomes a new creature. Old desires are replaced by new ones,
notably the desire to live for the Lord and please Him. If a
person cannot point to a time in her life when her thinking
and way of life were transformed, she might well question
whether she has ever truly been born again.

Vivian was enslaved by drugs, alcohol, and cigarettes.
Invited to church, she went—with a defiant attitude. She
donned her shortest miniskirt, took a swig of whiskey, and
sauntered up the church steps puffing on a cigarette.

Although the Christians had high standards on modesty
of dress, and they could smell the alcohol and smoke on
Vivian's breath, no one rebuked her. But Someone higher
up did. Hearing the gospel, she became convicted and
realized Christ had died for her. At the invitation, Vivian
ran down and fell before the altar.

Vivian's life has been transformed. Gone are the drugs,
alcohol, and cigarettes. Now she helps many come to her
Savior. If anyone shines forth the joy of the Lord, she does.
Oh, yes, the righteous can sing and rejoice!

36

Joy in God's Kingdom

BIBLE READING: Isaiah 35

They shall obtain joy and gladness, and sorrow and sighing shall flee away (v. 10).

Some of you are going through deep waters. Perhaps you are bedridden or have cancer, arthritis, or some other debility. Perhaps you are enduring a wretched homelife, racked with insecurity, fear, and heartache. All this talk of joy—how can you have joy in your circumstances?

God knows just where you are. He says gently and lovingly, "Strengthen ye the weak hands, and confirm the feeble knees. Say to them that are of a fearful heart, Be strong, fear not . . . God will come . . . and save you" (Isaiah 35: 3-4).

A day is coming, God says, when the blind shall see, the deaf shall hear, the lame person shall leap as a deer, and the tongue of the dumb shall shout for joy. The hand of the oppressor shall be lifted and shall be no more. The redeemed shall inherit the earth and shall delight themselves in the abundance of peace (Psalm 37:11).

We shall fellowship with our Lord in person. We shall have glorious new bodies like His—perfect, never ill or broken down. We shall receive rewards for faithfulness, and shall reign with Him in glory. No more sorrow, no more pain—God will wipe away all tears (Revelation 21: 4).

If you find it hard to have joy in this life, as a Christian you can still have God's deep joy in your heart because Christ has saved your soul and someday you will enjoy eternity with Him!

37

Joy in God's Comforts

BIBLE READING: Psalm 94:17-22

> In the multitude of my thoughts . . . thy comforts
> delight my soul (v. 19).

Like Christian in *The Pilgrim's Progress,* we sometimes
walk a distance from the River of God on stony places, feeling the flints sharp and rough beneath our feet. Attracted
to By-Path Meadow, we take what we think is the easy
way—only to fall into the crushing clutch of the grim giant,
DESPAIR. And off he drags us to Doubting Castle.

It is easy to become a prisoner in Doubting Castle when
our guard is down, or when we are feeling low physically or
emotionally. Like lashes of a torturing whip, our thoughts
assail us with fears, anxieties, and doubts about the future.
The old dragon in the moat does not help a bit by reminding
us of things to fret about. His darts get through because we
forgot our shield of faith.

The world's comforts mean little to us at a time like this,
but God has promised, "I will never leave thee, nor forsake
thee" (Hebrews 13:5). Though we be in the deepest dungeon of despair, our Lord is with us. No matter how tu-
multuous our thoughts, if we will be still and look to the
Lord, He will send His comforts to delight our souls. Delight our souls? At such a time? Yes.

He will remind us how He has taken care of us in the
past. He will show us a shiny shaft of sunlight from His
Word to remind us of His tender love. The dungeon door
will open, and out we will run into the full sunlight of God's
love, delighting in His comforts. On wings of joy we will
fly back to the River of God.

38

Joy in God's Creation

BIBLE READING: Job 38:4-7

O LORD, how manifold are thy works! in wisdom hast thou made them all: the earth is full of thy riches (Psalm 104:24).

I live in Greenville, South Carolina, in the foothills of the Great Smoky Mountains. On autumn days I revel in the beauty of the riot of color: the deep maroon of the dogwoods, the red gold of the maples, the dark green of the spruces. The sight so fills me with joy that I want to sing praises to the Lord.

Another time I will pick a flower and marvel at its intricate beauty, the perfection of its stamen and petals, and its fragrance. The wonder of the detail my heavenly Father has built in these small creations fills me with awe and joy.

One summer night while camping at a state park, Lori and I looked up at the dark sky and gloried in the myriads of stars.

I have taken a baby's tiny hand in mine and marveled at its perfection, beauty, and utility. I have studied the amazing design of our bodies, our organs, our ears, our eyes. The fact that our eyes have millions of cones to make them work properly has filled me with such awe for God that I have rejoiced in Him and His creation.

You can probably think of wonders of God's creation that have moved you. Why not meditate on them right now?

Isn't God beautiful? We miss some of His joy for us when we pass by His glorious creations day after day without noticing their beauty.

39

The Joy of Salvation

Bible Reading: Psalm 51:1-13

Restore unto me the joy of thy salvation (v. 12).

David committed what many consider the two worst sins: adultery and murder. But it does not appear from the biblical account that he was especially convicted. Perhaps he rationalized, as many do, and found excuses for himself. At any rate, we certainly know that his heart was not right with the Lord.

When Nathan the prophet faced David with his sins, their enormity hit him full force. Perhaps shortly after Nathan left, David fell to his knees before the Lord and cried the prayer found in Psalm 51.

One thing David prayed for was that God would restore the joy of salvation he had once known. He realized he had not had that joy for some time.

Are you enjoying the joy of your salvation? Or has it gotten lost in the shuffle of everyday living? Perhaps you were not aware it was missing until now. Remember when you had it, when you first gave your heart to Christ?

Not only big sins rob us of our joy of salvation. If we allow anything to come between us and God, we lose it. That is why it is so important to confess our shortcomings daily and ask His forgiveness and help in overcoming them. God is ready to forgive! He forgave David.

David did get his joy of salvation back; we know, for God has used him to inspire believers down through the ages with his prayer in Psalm 51. If you long for the joy of your salvation to be restored, pray the same prayer David did.

40

Joy in God's Goodness

BIBLE READING: 1 Chronicles 16:28-36

O taste and see that the LORD is good: blessed is
the man that trusteth in him (Psalm 34:8).

If we would really *taste* and see how good the Lord is,
we would be filled with joy! What does *taste* mean? To
savor, to relish, to enjoy. When you taste fried chicken and
chew it slowly to savor it, you are deriving enjoyment!

Matthew Henry said, "Let God's goodness be rolled under
the tongue as a sweet morsel. We must see that he is a
beautiful being, and delight in the contemplation of his
infinite perfections." When we taste and see that God is
good, we cannot help but trust Him; in the trusting we are
blessed.

We tasted of the Lord when we received Christ as our
Savior. He became real to us. His goodness became personal as the burden of sin rolled off.

After we are with the Lord for awhile, we sometimes forget how good He is. We drop our shield of faith a bit, and
the devil gets through with his fiery darts of doubts and
fears (Ephesians 6:16). Then we doubt God's goodness,
even as Eve did when Satan got through to her. We lose our
joy when we doubt and fear.

Come, trust in the Lord with all your heart, and do not
lean on your own understanding (Proverbs 3:5-6). God
is good! Look up verses on God's goodness. Meditate on
them. Recall God's goodness and mercy to you. Never mind
things you cannot understand. Someday we shall understand all things.

41

Joy in God's House

BIBLE READING: Acts 2:41-47

I was glad when they said unto me, Let us go into
the house of the LORD (Psalm 122:1).

We who live in a free land may take the privilege of
churchgoing for granted. Many Christians even begrudge
God one or two hours on Sunday morning. But what a joy
it should be to gather with His people to worship Him and
learn more of His Word!

In the Soviet Union, numerous churches have been closed,
and many of the buildings have been made museums. Offi-
cially recognized churches are under the heavy hand of the
atheistic government. Underground churches are persecuted.

In his book *Underground Saints,* Richard Wurmbrand
tells how a group of Russian Christians risked their free-
dom to meet for worship. Standing during the entire service,
they filled a darkened, low-ceilinged room. Streaks of sweat
ran down their tired faces. "With all your heart," said their
pastor, "rest your hope with God and do not rely on your
mind!"

We Christians in free lands can go to well-lighted, air-
conditioned churches with comfortable pews for services
throughout the week. We can freely take our children to
Sunday school, delight in fellowship with one another, not
fearing that someone will report us for worshiping, witnessing, or passing out tracts.

Think how blessed we are to be able to go to God's house
and fellowship and worship with His people. Let the joy
of that privilege warm your heart.

42

Joy of the Desolate

BIBLE READING: 2 Corinthians 1:2-7

For I will turn their mourning into joy, and will
comfort them (Jeremiah 31:13).

Have you been feeling desolate because of the loss of a
loved one, the breakup of your marriage, or the wayward-
ness of one of your children? Turn to the Lord right now
for comfort. He is the best Comforter there is!

Jesus understands our every heartache and temptation.
God's Word says:

> For we have not an high priest which cannot be touched
> with the feeling of our infirmities; but was in all points
> tempted like as we are, yet without sin. Let us there-
> fore come boldly unto the throne of grace, that we may
> obtain mercy, and find grace to help in time of need
> (Hebrews 4:15-16).

In John 14-16, Jesus promised His disciples He would
send to them the Comforter, the Holy Spirit, who imparts
to each committed disciple Christ's peace and joy. Through
the Spirit, Christ is always with us (John 14:17-18).

Why do we continue to be desolate? Because we have not
followed God's plain directions in the Bible. God tells us to
come boldly to obtain His help. Instead, we allow ourselves
to remain so depressed that we think we cannot even pray.
When we get into that state, all we need to do is just look
up and cry, "Help me, Father!" The Lord does not expect
fancy prayers; all He wants is faith in Him.

God is the God of all comfort, who comforts us in every
tribulation, so that we may be able to comfort others. In
that comfort is the seed of joy, for joy comes when we know
Someone loves us very much!

43

Joy in Forgiving God

BIBLE READING: Romans 8:22-28

Trust in the LORD with all thine heart; and lean not unto thine own understanding (Proverbs 3: 5).

Some of the world's most miserable people cannot seem to forgive God. Some cruel blow struck and crushed them; blaming God, they put Him out of their lives.

Lorelei lost her first child in infancy. She had grown up believing that God was a God of judgment, and she blamed Him for the loss of her baby. "I couldn't think of what I had done to deserve such punishment," she told me.

Lorelei turned from God and stopped going to church. Her marriage ended in divorce. At twenty-one she became a stripteaser, and for a number of years she lived a sinful life. Then God sent someone to witness to her and show her His love. As she realized God really loved her, she yielded her heart to Christ. Joy filled her soul as the bitterness was washed away.

Some people blame God if their children go astray, or if their mates desert them, or if they are stricken with a painful or fatal illness. But they hurt themselves most by such animosity toward God.

Many Christians, however, have endured terrible blows and have trusted the Lord to work all things together for good. And He has. Not only that, but such Christians have been used greatly of God to His glory. And they often have known a special closeness to God. How sweet to know that nothing comes into our lives except through God's loving hand!

44

Joy in Loving God

BIBLE READING: 1 John 4:10-19

I love the LORD, because he hath heard my voice
and my supplications (Psalm 116:1).

As I began research for this devotion, I meditated on my
love for God and His love for me. Joy filled me as I dwelled
on these thoughts. There is wonderful joy in loving Him.
Meditate for a few minutes and see what happens.

When we truly love the Lord, we want to show Him our
love. Hebrews 6:10 (NIV) says, "God is not unjust; he
will not forget your work and the love you have shown him
as you have helped his people and continue to help them."

We experience real joy when we help God's children by
listening; comforting; counseling; praying with them; visiting; providing food, clothing, or money; reading God's
Word with them; or showing God's love in other ways.

When my husband was a ministerial student, I went every
week to a hospital to visit the sick. A severely crippled hy-
drocephalic man in a wheelchair asked me to read the Bible
to him one night. After that I visited him every week. I
cannot describe the joy I felt when I saw his face light up
at my appearance. How happy I was to be able to bring
some joy into this dear saint's life—and what a blessing he
was to me!

I went to that hospital because I loved the Lord and felt
led to express that love by visiting and encouraging His
people. But joy in loving and serving God is not just for
me. It is for every believer.

45

Joy in Forgiving Yourself

BIBLE READING: John 8:1-11

Forgetting those things which are behind, and
reaching forth unto those things which are before,
I press toward the mark for the prize of the high
calling of God in Christ Jesus (Philippians 3:13-
14).

It is impossible for us to have the joy of the Lord if we
cannot forgive ourselves.

When I was teaching at a Christian writers' conference,
a young woman made an appointment to speak to me about
writing; but it turned out to be a personal counseling session.

"I'm divorced," Jackie told me. "I have two little children,
and now they have been robbed of their father because of
me. I know it's my fault our marriage went on the rocks,
and I'm so miserable about it day in and day out that I just
don't know what to do!"

Jackie's husband had remarried, I learned, so she could
not be reconciled with him. She had often sought forgiveness from the Lord for her mistakes, and she knew she was a
child of God. But she still could not forgive herself.

"Jackie," I said, "if God forgives us, shouldn't we be willing to forgive ourselves?" I reminded her of how Jesus
dealt with the woman taken in adultery. When all her
accusers felt too ashamed of themselves to condemn her,
Jesus said, "Neither do I condemn thee: go, and sin no
more" (John 8:11).

We cannot undo the past, but we can make the present
and future glorious by forgetting what is behind and press-
ing toward the high calling of God in Christ. Forgive yourself for past mistakes, even as Jesus has.

46

Joy in Loving Yourself

BIBLE READING: Jeremiah 1:4-8

Thou shalt love thy neighbor as thyself (Matthew 22:29).

Many think the above Scripture verse only teaches that we should love our neighbors. But as I read that verse recently, I realized the two words on the end carry an additional teaching: "as thyself." Many cannot truly love others because they do not love themselves. Their attitude often results in a king-size inferiority complex, which in turn affects their relationships with others.

A person with such a complex may take out his anger and frustration with himself on others by using a device psychologists call "projection" to relieve himself; he will accuse others of the same faults he has. He may readily hurt and offend others; but because of his inferiority complex, he will be supersensitive himself.

Basically self-centered, he desires to love himself. But because he cannot respect himself, he hates himself. The conflict that hate causes in his heart keeps him from joy. The conflict it causes with others not only stops him from having joy, but it also makes everyone living with him miserable.

If that is our problem, how can we outgrow it? As Christians we can remind ourselves that we are children of the King. When we start dwelling on our inadequacies or failures, let's think about how much the Lord wants to do in us and through us if we will yield our lives to Him. Let's think about how much He loves us, and that He has a wonderful purpose for our lives. Let's think of Him, not of ourselves. Our God is able to make each of us worthwhile.

47

Joy in Forgiving Others

BIBLE READING: Matthew 18:21-35

If ye forgive men their trespasses, your heavenly
Father will also forgive you (Matthew 6:14).

Two women who worked together in a church disputed
one day over the way something should be done. Hurtful
words were said hastily in front of others. Each woman felt
she had been humiliated by the other.

After she had cooled off, Pat regretted the whole episode
and sent a note of apology. But Marianne felt she never
could overlook what had been said. When her grudge toward Pat eventually hurt the church's work, the pastor suggested she resign. Thus Marianne found the Lord's mercy
had deserted her in that situation. Jesus said, "If ye forgive
not men their trespasses, neither will your Father forgive
your trespasses" (Matthew 6:15). Marianne did not lose her
salvation, as some believe this verse teaches. Rather, God
allowed her to reap the full consequences of what she had
sown.

When we refuse to truly forgive someone, it is impossible
for us to have joy. That grudge rankles bitterly in our hearts,
especially whenever we see that person or hear his name.
Lack of a forgiving spirit in our hearts separates us from
our Lord. It really isn't worth holding onto, is it?

God is able to help us love even the unlovely. He can put
a forgiving spirit in our hearts, if we will let Him. After all,
He loved us even when we were sinners who had no time
for Him and disobeyed His laws. He forgives us all the
time, even though we often grieve Him and let Him down.

48

Joy in Loving Others

BIBLE READING: 1 Corinthians 13:1-7

Beloved, if God so loved us, we ought also to love
one another (1 John 4:11).

In Romans 13:8, God tells us, "Owe no man any thing,
but to love one another; for he that loveth another hath fulfilled the law." If we truly love others, we will not kill
them, steal, bear false witness, or covet what is theirs. We
will, as Jesus said, love our neighbors as ourselves.

How do we like people to speak to us or treat us? Kindly,
patiently, with understanding? How would our relationships
be if we lived by 1 Corinthians 13? We would be a lot hap-
pier and have more joy in our hearts.

After Betty came to know the Lord, she was completely
changed. Her husband, rebelling at her new religious zeal,
became harder to live with. She responded by showing
him love—being sweet and considerate, mowing the grass,
washing the car, and vacuuming the swimming pool, so he
could have more free time. Jack Matthews could not resist
such love. He also gave his heart to Christ. Eventually he
became dean of men at Columbia Bible College.

If Betty had responded to Jack's attitude with a similar
attitude, she would have been miserable. But she had the joy
of seeing him turn to Christ.

We can apply this principle of love to our relationships
with everyone we know. We will not only have joy in our
hearts because we know we are pleasing our Lord, but we
will have joy because of our greater peace and harmony.

49

Joy in God's Loving-kindness

BIBLE READING: Psalm 107:1-15

It is a good thing . . . to sing praises unto thy name,
O most High: to shew forth thy lovingkindness in
the morning (Psalm 92:1-2).

For a number of years Janice was married to a paranoid
man with manic-depressive tendencies, and she lived a miserable
life full of turmoil and abuse. She was a Christian
and continually cried unto the Lord. But still the life she
led was hard to bear at times. Finally God delivered her
from her hades on earth.

She became one of the most joyful Christians I know,
daily rejoicing in God's loving-kindness. The Lord has
provided for all her needs in a remarkable way, and opened
up unique opportunities for her to serve Him. Because of all
her trials, she has been able to comfort and encourage many
others.

I think we have to go through some hard places to really
appreciate God's loving-kindness. If everything always went
well, we might take His loving-kindness for granted. But
when things go wrong and we see how He helps us, how
grateful we are for His tender care and concern.

Many Christians seem unaware of God's loving-kindness
and take His blessings for granted. Consequently, they do
not thank Him. How many further blessings might they
miss because they show no gratitude? Conversely, how many
additional blessings do those persons receive who praise and
thank God for His loving-kindness?

If you praise God for His loving-kindness, you will have
joy.

53

50

Joy in Christ's Assurance

BIBLE READING: Romans 8:35-39

These things have I spoken unto you, that my joy might remain in you, and that your joy might be full (John 15:11).

It is wonderfully assuring to us who follow Christ to realize that He knows us. For Jesus said, "My sheep hear my voice, and I know them, and they follow me; and I give unto them eternal life; and they shall never perish, neither shall any man pluck them out of my hand" (John 10:27-28).

This comforting assurance that our Lord Jesus Christ holds us in His omnipotent hand brings full joy into our hearts if we truly believe it. And how does this full joy remain in us day after day? Jesus gave the recipe in John 15:10-12: "If ye keep my commandments, ye shall abide in my love. . . . This is my commandment, That ye love one another, as I have loved you."

How reassuring are God's promises in Romans 8:35-39, that nothing can separate us from the love of Christ! *Nothing!* Think about that. He loves us so much that He holds us firmly in His hand. He knows all the trials and tribulations we will encounter. We are His lambs; He knows us by name; and He will keep us safely in His hand.

If God's hand were that of just a man, we might have reason to fear. But when His omnipotent hand holds us, we can have joy every morning!

51

Joy in God's Peace

Bible Reading: John 14:23-27

And the peace of God, which passeth all understanding, shall keep your hearts and minds through Christ Jesus (Philippians 4:7).

A year after my husband and I turned our lives over to God, my mind was occupied with troubles. My husband had quit his well-paying job. How were we going to pay the bills? We had payments due on a new home, car, and furniture. Then I ran into a lawyer's car with our car! Shortly after, we received an exorbitant bill we could not pay. When the lawyer sued us, I really worried.

The next Sunday our pastor used Philippians 4:7 as his benediction. *Peace that passeth understanding?* I puzzled. *How does a Christian get that, especially when she has so many problems?* When I got home, I read the verse in its context. The key is Philippians 4:6, "Do not be anxious about anything, but in everything, by prayer and petition, with thanksgiving, present your requests to God" (NIV).

I believed it and tried it. It worked! God's peace filled my heart as I committed our problems to Him. I was so relieved! Almost immediately God laid it on my heart to call the lawyer and explain our circumstances. "Oh well, then," he said, "I'll settle for twenty dollars." And my husband soon found another job.

God hears us when we come in simple faith to Him; but if our trust in Him wavers, the Bible says we will receive nothing (James 1:6-7). If we have complete faith that He will take care of everything, we will have peace with joy— and He will take care of everything!

52

Joy for the Brokenhearted

BIBLE READING: Luke 4:16-21

He ... sent me to heal the brokenhearted (v. 18).

Has your heart been broken, and are you wondering how you can have joy with such an ache filling your whole being? You can! God sent something into my life that broke my heart, so I know it is possible. It is easy to speak glibly about joy when you are happy and content. Anyone can be cheerful then. The test of Christianity is that we who love Jesus can learn to rejoice even in circumstances that tear up our hearts!

Jesus said His Father had sent Him to heal the brokenhearted. Do you believe that? Will you accept it now? Kneel and ask Him to pick up the pieces of your broken heart and mold them together with His love. Then you will have a new heart filled with the compassion and love of God for others, as well as so much more love for the One who cares enough to heal you.

Come, even while your heart still aches; rejoice in the Lord. That is one antidote for a broken heart. In everything give thanks—even in that thing that has broken your heart. God dearly loves you, and He will not allow anything to come into your life that will not work for your ultimate good. He is going to use that heartache to enrich your life with understanding, with concern for others, and with the desire to let Him use you as a comforter.

Now meditate on God's love, on the realization of how greatly He must love you and want to use you for His glory, to have trusted you with this trial!

53

Joy in God's Fatherhood

BIBLE READING: Romans 8:14-21

And will be a Father unto you, and ye shall be
my sons and daughters, saith the Lord Almighty
(2 Corinthians 6:18).

One of the most glorious Bible truths is in John 1:12:
"But as many as received him, to them gave he power to become the sons of God, even to them that believe on his
name." Contrary to a currently popular theory, God is not
the Father of all. He is the Creator of all, but not the Father.
Jesus told the deceitful Pharisees, "Ye are of your father the
devil" (John 8:44).

But even some Pharisees came to know God as their
Father. When Saul, the great persecutor, yielded to Christ,
he became God's son, Paul. Later he wrote to the Christians
at Rome, "Ye have received the Spirit of adoption, whereby
we cry, Abba, Father. The Spirit itself beareth witness with
our spirit, that we are the children of God" (Romans 8:15-
16).

Abba is a Syriac word meaning "father," and Jesus Himself prayed saying, "Abba, Father" (Mark 14:36). Why
both? According to Matthew Henry, "It denotes an affectionate endearing importunity, and a believing stress laid
upon the relation. Little children, begging of their parents,
can say little but *Father, Father,* and that is rhetoric enough."

If you are God's child through faith in Christ, why not
look to Him right now and say, "Abba, Father," or "Father,
Father"? Then be still and glory in that fact that He is your
loving Father, and you are His child.

54

Joy in God's Incarnation

BIBLE READING: John 1:1-14

And without controversy great is the mystery of godliness: God was manifest in the flesh, justified in the Spirit, seen of angels, preached unto the Gentiles, believed on in the world, received up into glory (1 Timothy 3:16).

Isn't it amazing that God would love us so much that He would actually become a man? Can you imagine giving your life willingly as a guinea pig to save others? This analogy cannot begin to portray what God did.

God the Son never became an angel. He humbled Himself and was made in the likeness of man (Philippians 2:5-8). "But we see Jesus, who was made a little lower than the angels for the suffering of death, crowned with glory and honour; that he by the grace of God should taste death for every man" (Hebrews 2:9).

Old Testament prophecy also affirms Jesus was God in the flesh: "For unto us a child is born, unto us a son is given . . . and his name shall be called . . . The Mighty God" (Isaiah 9:6).

So, out of love for us, God became a man in order to die the most excruciating death ever devised for man. Not only was it physically excruciating (see Psalm 22), but it was spiritually excruciating. For the only time in eternity, God the Father was separated from God the Son (Mark 15:34) because of our sins!

Now our God is a resurrected man, interceding for us in heaven. He understands our problems, our heartaches, our temptations. Think about God's incarnation and allow the joy of His love to fill your heart.

55

Joy in Jesus

BIBLE READING: Philippians 2:5-11

They worshipped him, and returned to Jerusalem
with great joy (Luke 24:52).

We can have joy in God's incarnation; we also can have
joy in Jesus, which is a more personal thing.

What a friend we have in Jesus! "There is a friend that
sticketh closer than a brother" (Proverbs 18:24). That is
Jesus. Our family may let us down, but Jesus never will.
Family and friends may misunderstand or take offense, but
Jesus understands our every weakness and is always ready
to forgive and help us. Earthly friends may prove untrue,
but Jesus says, "I am with you alway" (Matthew 28:20).

What a Savior we have in Jesus! Matthew 1:21 says,
"And she shall bring forth a son, and thou shalt call his
name JESUS: for he shall save his people from their sins."
Jesus does not just save us from having to pay the penalty
for our sins in eternity, but He saves us from our sins *now*.
Romans 6:14 says, "For sin shall not have dominion over
you: for ye are not under the law, but under grace." Is it
not something to rejoice about the fact that we no longer
need to be slaves to sin? Christ gives us the power by His
Spirit to live victorious, godly lives—abundant lives that
allow us to have daily joy.

What a Master we have in Jesus! He is surely worth following to the ends of the world! The Bible says, "His banner over me was love" (Song of Solomon 2:4). Let us look
up at that banner of love, and at the Captain whose banner it
is, and determine to be good soldiers for Him who has
chosen us (2 Timothy 2:3-4).

56

Joy in the Holy Spirit

BIBLE READING: Galatians 5:22-25

For the kingdom of God is not eating and drinking, but righteousness and peace and joy in the Holy Spirit (Romans 14:17, NASB).

When we first yield our lives fully to the Lord, the Holy Spirit fills our hearts and we bubble over with joy. Jesus said, "If any man is thirsty, let him come to Me and drink. He who believes in Me, as the Scripture said, 'From his innermost being shall flow rivers of living water' " (John 7:37-38, NASB). John explained, "But this spake he of the Spirit, which they that believe on him should receive" (John 7:39). So one sure sign that the Holy Spirit indwells us is that we cannot keep the Good News about Christ and salvation to ourselves (Acts 1:8). From our inmost being flows living water that can bring eternal life to others. They not only hear it from us, but also they see it in our radiant joy.

Another sure sign that the Holy Spirit indwells us is that we will want to glorify Jesus—not our church, our religion, some mere man, or ourselves. Jesus said of the Comforter, "He shall testify of me. He shall glorify me" (John 15:26; 16:14). So it will give you joy to glorify Jesus, too.

The Holy Spirit guides and teaches us (John 14:26; 16:13). Isn't it a joy to know that we need not walk in darkness as the children of this world do? Through the Holy Spirit we may know the truth, the right way to go, the right decision to make. He also gives us the power to overcome, the power to live godly lives (Galatians 5:16). Just that realization should give us joy!

60

57

Joy in God's Faithfulness

BIBLE READING: Psalm 89:1-5

Great is thy faithfulness (Lamentations 3:23).

When I was twenty-six and my husband thirty-three, he came to know Christ as his Savior. Two years later he felt called by God to preach. We knew this meant that he should go to Bible college to prepare for the ministry.

Suddenly the new home and car we had waited for so long seemed of no account. My husband said, "I am going to put out the fleece. This week I will tell only three people that I want to sell our car. If God wants me to prepare for the ministry, I believe the car will be sold by the end of the week."

Two of the men Al told already had good cars. The third was a missionary who had just returned from the field, a man whom he had no reason to believe had any money. On Friday the missionary came and said he felt led to buy the car with some money he had received unexpectedly.

We put our house up for sale, but the realtors told us the market was not good. Within the month the house was sold. We moved to South Carolina so Al could attend Columbia Bible College, and within a week I had a job.

During the years of schooling, the Lord continually provided our needs. He supplied us both with work; He supplied us with homes where the rent was very reasonable; He always supplied the tuition on time. We learned in our preparation for the Lord's service how faithful He was!

Recall God's faithfulness to you. It will give you joy!

58

Shine with Joy

BIBLE READING: Jeremiah 9:23-24

That, according as it is written, He that glorieth,
let him glory in the Lord (1 Corinthians 1:31).

The above quotation in 1 Corinthians is taken from Jeremiah 9:23, where the Hebrew word used for "glory" is *halal,* "to shine" or "to celebrate." The Greek word for "glory" in Corinthians is *kauchaomai,* which means "joy" or "rejoice." Since the verses were connected by God, we can say that "to glory" is "to shine with joy" because of the Lord.

The Christians in the early church must have shone with joy. They ate "with gladness and singleness of heart, praising God, and having favour with all the people. And the Lord added to the church daily" (Acts 2:46-47). They were so dynamic, such radiant lights for Christ, that it was said of them, "These . . . have turned the world upside down" (Acts 17:6).

What would happen in our churches today if more Christians were like those early saints, full of the Holy Spirit and shining for joy? Would not revival come, and would not our churches soon be packed to the doors?

The Lord, through Jeremiah, said that we should glory because we understand and know Him in all His lovingkindness, judgment, and righteousness. If we truly glory in God, we shall be like Him, for we shall see Him as He is. People see God when we are shining for Him. Joy and shining go together like sun and sunlight. So today shine with joy for Jesus!

59

Joy in God's Marvelous Light

BIBLE READING: Ephesians 2:1-10

But ye are a chosen generation, a royal priesthood, an holy nation, a peculiar people; that ye should shew forth the praises of him who hath called you out of darkness into his marvellous light (1 Peter 2:9).

Have you ever felt awed by the fact that we Christians were chosen "before the foundation of the world, that we should be holy and without blame before him in love" (Ephesians 1:4)? Yes, God, being omniscient, knew even before He made the world which of us would receive His Son as Savior. He "predestinated us unto the adoption of children by Jesus Christ to himself" (Ephesians 1:5). That wondrous realization should fill our hearts with joy.

Besides ordaining us to become His children, God also has made us His priests to offer the spiritual sacrifices of prayer, praise, and good works, and to intercede for our fellowmen and help them come to know Him.

We belong especially to God, the Creator of the universe. The Greek word used for "peculiar" carries the meaning of a purchased possession, and certainly God did purchase us at a tremendous cost: His lifeblood. Since we belong so especially to God, He is vitally concerned about every detail of our lives.

When we receive Christ, we who were dead in trespasses and sins become alive. God opens our spiritual eyes and we see things we never saw before (1 Corinthians 2:12-16). We who were in darkness have been called into God's marvelous light. Let us rejoice in Christ!

60

Meditation for Joy

BIBLE READING: Psalm 119:97-104

Let the words of my mouth, and the meditation of
my heart, be acceptable in thy sight, O LORD, my
strength, and my redeemer (Psalm 19:14).

In recent years, transcendental meditation has become a
popular practice, so much so that courses have been offered
in various schools. This Hindu religious practice, however,
may be dangerous, according to former teachers of TM.
In any case, it centers in the worship of Hindu gods. Certainly no Christian should dabble in this kind of meditation!

Perhaps the interest in meditation has sprung from our
busy world. The need to "get away from it all" has increased. Whether we are housewives and mothers who work
at home or outside the home, we might often feel harried
and hurried. This may drive our nerves up the wall and our
voices up twenty decibels! We need to get away, if only for
a few minutes.

What better way to get away than to return to the biblical
concept of meditation? If non-Christians can spend thirty
minutes meditating, why can't we spend a few minutes to
allow God to give rest to our souls?

The psalmist said he would meditate on God's precepts,
testimonies, Word, and glorious works. In addition to meditating on those things, we should think about our Lord's
promises, faithfulness, and love. This will draw us closer to
Him and allow His gentle and peaceable Spirit to fill our
spirits. Our nerves will relax and we will have joy and
sweet dispositions again.

61

Joy in God's Guidance

BIBLE READING: Psalm 32:7-11

He will be our guide even unto death (Psalm 48: 14).

When I worked in Tennessee, a closed-bid sale was held on used office equipment. I felt led to buy an electric typewriter, and one of the men from my office went with me to help me make a bid.

We found a machine that seemed to be in good condition. "What do you think I ought to bid?" I asked the man.

"Oh, about $83," he suggested.

I sent up a quick prayer. Then I felt led to put in a bid for $84.07.

Later I was informed that my bid had been the highest, and the typewriter was mine. From a list of bids sent me, I saw that two similar typewriters had gone to a man who had bid $84.06! I have used this machine for fourteen years in writing eleven books and hundreds of articles. I really rejoiced in the Lord's guidance when I realized I had gotten my typewriter by a penny's margin!

I have had many other occasions in which to rejoice in His guidance. Isn't it wonderful how He leads us, His children, in all our problems and decisions, big and small, when we look to Him for His guidance?

How many mistakes we can avoid if we will consult the Lord! He will share His wisdom with us in many ways if we will only seek it! Psalm 32 says God will guide us with His eye (v. 8). It also says, "Be glad in the LORD, and rejoice, ye righteous: and shout for joy, all ye that are upright in heart" (v. 11). Certainly God's sure guidance will cause us to shout for joy!

62

Rejoice in Christ Jesus

BIBLE READING: Philippians 3:1-10

Rejoice in Christ Jesus (v. 3).

Why do you suppose Philippians 3:3 does not just say, "Rejoice in Christ" or "Rejoice in Jesus"? Why do you think the inspired Word of God uses both of His names here? Mark it well, if the Holy Spirit led the writer to use certain words, He had a reason!

Christ, the name of our incarnate God, is synonymous with the Hebrew *Messiah.* The Messiah was to be the Savior of His people (Isaiah 53:5-6). God tells us through Isaiah, "I, even I, am the LORD; and beside me there is no saviour" (43:11). So who is this great Messiah but God Himself? And only God Himself, the sinless Lamb whose sacrifice could be infinite, could pay the price for the sins of all of us who trust in Him for salvation.

We can rejoice in the truth that God the Son loved us so much that He left heaven's glory to become a lowly Servant. Isn't it marvelous to be loved that much? Even if no one else loves us, He does!

And then there's *Jesus,* His name as a man. "Thou shalt call his name JESUS: for he shall save his people from their sins" (Matthew 1:21). Jesus—Savior. In order to save us, our Redeemer had to be both God and man. He had to be subject to the same temptations as we are, yet be without sin (Hebrews 4:15).

We cannot truly rejoice in Christ Jesus unless we realize He is our personal Savior. Have you acknowledged Him as that? If not, why not do it now?

63

Joy in God's Love

BIBLE READING: Luke 15:11-24

We love him, because he first loved us (1 John 4:19).

Do you love the Lord? If so, why? No doubt it is because first you realized His love for you. But our human love falls far short of God's love. We readily love those who love us, "but God commendeth his love toward us, in that, while we were yet sinners, Christ died for us" (Romans 5:8).

Elizabeth Barrett Browning wrote, "How do I love thee? Let me count the ways." How does God love us? Let us count the ways.

"For God so loved the world, that he gave his only begotten Son, that whosoever believeth in him should not perish, but have everlasting life" (John 3:16).

"Yea, I have loved thee with an everlasting love: therefore with lovingkindness have I drawn thee" (Jeremiah 31:3).

"Blessed be the God and Father of our Lord Jesus Christ, who hath blessed us with all spiritual blessings in heavenly places in Christ" (Ephesians 1:3).

"The Spirit itself beareth witness with our spirit, that we are the children of God: and if children, then heirs; heirs of God, and joint-heirs with Christ" (Romans 8:16-17).

"Eye hath not seen, nor ear heard, neither have entered into the heart of man, the things which God hath prepared for them that love him" (1 Corinthians 2:9).

When God adopts us, we are actually *born* of His Spirit. He becomes part of us and we of Him. That is how much God loves us. Rejoice in His love!

64

Joy in Answered Prayers

BIBLE READING: John 15:7-16

Hitherto have ye asked nothing in my name: ask,
and ye shall receive, that your joy may be full
(John 16:24).

One of the sweetest sources of joy comes from answered
prayer. The Lord has given me a prayer ministry in my
church, and frequently someone comes to me with a special
request. I jot it down so that I can bring it to the Lord
again and again in the days that follow.

Nearly every week someone shares with me how the Lord
has answered our prayers for a particular burden. That is
when joy fills my heart!

A mother asked me to pray for her teenage daughter who
was involved with an unsaved divorced man in his early
thirties. We prayed. Two months later the daughter was
going steady with a fine, young Christian.

Two important requirements for getting prayer answered
are: stay right with the Lord, and believe. Jesus said, "Therefore I say unto you, What things soever ye desire, when ye
pray, believe that ye receive them, and ye shall have them"
(Mark 11:24). Do you believe Him? Then claim His
promise!

Jesus' qualification for the promise is that we must forgive everyone (Mark 11:25). Examine your heart and
make sure you bear no grudge and that all is as right as you
can make it with others. Then pray about everything you
are concerned about. I pray about even the smallest problems. God's Spirit indwells Christians, and He can help
and guide us in everything!

65

Joy in Unanswered Prayer

BIBLE READING: Psalm 23

Though he slay me, yet will I trust in him (Job 13:15).

A mother was deeply concerned about her son. He had never received Christ as his Savior, and he was in a high-living crowd. He drank and ran around, and his mother suspected he might be doing something illegal.

"Lord, please don't let my boy get into trouble with the law," she pleaded. "Oh, please, help him to be saved!"

One night the police came and took her son to jail. "O Father, I prayed You would keep him out of jail!" the mother wept. But realizing how unfair she was for blaming the Lord for her son's misdeeds and consequent incarceration, she pleaded that the Lord would use the calamity to bring her son to Christ.

I think that was just what the Lord had in mind by allowing her son to be caught. As he sat in jail, he became convicted of his sinfulness and lost condition. Thinking of the heartache he was causing his mother, he recalled some of the Scripture she had quoted in seeking to point him to Christ. In the middle of the night, he knelt beside his bunk. "O Lord, I'm such a sinner!" he cried. "Please forgive me, and save me for Jesus' sake!"

So because that mother's first prayer was not answered as she had hoped, the second prayer *was* answered! When that young man got out of jail, he went to Bible school; now he teaches at a Bible college.

There is joy in knowing that God answers prayer, and also in having confidence in Him that when He does not answer as we desire, He knows what is best!

66

Joy in God's Strength

BIBLE READING: Isaiah 41:10-13

The LORD is my strength and song (Exodus 15:2).

Ruth had a happy marriage and loved her husband. One day she was visited by some grave-looking friends. "Ruth, we don't know how to tell you this," one said hesitantly, "but Lee was killed instantly this morning."

Ruth's hands flew to her face and she uttered a little cry. "Excuse me," she stammered, "I think I'd like to be alone for a moment!" In her bedroom, she cried softly, "What shall I do, Lord? How shall I pray? Please, help me!"

She snatched up her Bible and opened it at random. The words of a verse leaped out at her: "Likewise the Spirit also helpeth our infirmities: for we know not what we should pray for as we ought: but the Spirit itself maketh intercession for us with groanings which cannot be uttered" (Romans 8:26).

As this message from God sank into her consciousness, she felt a strange and wonderful strength she had never known. *Lee was ready to go,* she thought, *and now he is safe with our precious Lord!* God's strength helped Ruth to be a comfort to friends and family in their bereavement.

Rejoice that God says, "Fear thou not; for I am with thee: . . . I will strengthen thee; yea, I will help thee" (Isaiah 41:10). We need not fear the future, for God's strength and help will be with us through every trial.

Moses linked the fact that God was his strength and his song. Recall how God has strengthened you, and sing a song of joy and praise.

67

Joy in the Bridegroom

BIBLE READING: Song of Solomon 2:1-4

My beloved is mine, and I am his (Song of Solomon 2:16).

The Song of Solomon is a vivid word picture of the love and relationship that exist between Christ and His church. Believers are the fair virgin Christ loves and longs for. If our relationship with Him is right, we will feel that way about Him.

The Song of Solomon says His banner over us is love (2:4). When a city is taken, the conqueror sets up his standard over it. When Christ takes our hearts out of Satan's realm, He sets His love banner over us (Ephesians 2:1-7). We are His purchased possession; we belong to Him (1 Corinthians 6:19-20).

Even when we disappoint or grieve Him, His banner over us still is *love,* for He is always faithful. If we lack His peace and joy, it is not because He does not want us to have it. He always stands patiently at our heart's door waiting for our erring hearts to return to Him (Revelation 3:20).

When we go through deep waters, His banner over us still is *love.* He is in the water with us. But often our thoughts are so filled with our misery that we do not see Him waiting to be our comfort, strength, and all we need.

When a girl is about to be married, her beloved is in her thoughts constantly and she eagerly looks forward to seeing him. The sight of him fills her with joy; the thought of belonging to him thrills her to the core of her being.

Jesus is our Beloved. He wants to be our constant joy.

68

Shout for Joy!

BIBLE READING: Psalm 5

Let them ever shout for joy (v. 11).

When was the last time you shouted for joy in the Lord? If you did that in the average church today, probably you would knock half the sleepers off their pews, and a deacon would quickly call the local mental health clinic!

Granted, things must be done decently and in order in the church. But sometimes I wonder if most saints will be ready for heaven. Revelation 7:9-10 says, "A great multitude . . . stood before the throne . . . clothed with white robes . . . and cried with a loud voice, saying, Salvation to our God which sitteth upon the throne, and unto the Lamb." Yes, there will be joyful shouts of praise to God and our Savior in heaven (Revelation 19:6-7).

Psalm 47:1 says, "O clap your hands, all ye people; shout unto God with the voice of triumph." Ezra 3:11 tells how the happy children of Israel shouted and praised the Lord.

Like most of you, I would be embarrassed to death to shout out for joy during a church service. But sometimes I am so full of the joy of the Lord that I just leap around in my heart and shout silent praises to Him there. And I sing the hymns of praise to Him with all my heart. So what if some of those around me hardly open their mouths? That is their loss!

If you are alone at home and become filled with the joy of the Lord, stand up and shout for joy! Then you will begin to know what praise is all about.

69

Wine of Joy

BIBLE READING: Isaiah 55:1-9

Come, buy wine and milk without money and
without price! (v. 1).

Isaiah cried out a free offer to all who thirst after happiness in the favor of God to come and buy wine and milk
without money. What did he mean in this offer made only
to those who had no money?

When we come to God, we have to see ourselves as He,
the Holy God, sees us: unclean, unworthy, with nothing to
commend us. We cannot buy the new wine of joy imparted
by the Holy Spirit through spiritual rebirth with an earthly
payment or act. Salvation is priceless; it was bought with
Christ's blood, which was shed for our sins. We can only
"buy" it by appropriating that payment. Only when we
come to Jesus and invite Him into our lives are we filled
with the new wine of joy.

The milk, also priceless, is the milk of God's Word, the
sustenance of spiritual life (1 Peter 2:2). We cannot buy
it with education or intellect. "But the natural man receiveth not the things of the Spirit of God: . . . neither can
he know them, because they are spiritually discerned" (1 Corinthians 2:14). That is why the Bible is like a closed book
to so many and why it is so frequently misinterpreted.
When we are born into God's family, the Holy Spirit enters
our hearts and opens our eyes to spiritual truths.

By abiding in the Lord we will have His wine of joy and
milk of nourishment for our souls.

70

Joy in God Our Fortress

BIBLE READING: Psalm 71:1-5

For thou art my rock and my fortress (v. 3).

Did you ever feel desperate for a place to run to and hide and feel protected? At the top of Psalm 71 in my Bible, I penned the dates of two days I felt that way and the psalm reminded me who my fortress was.

The Lord is our rock, fortress, deliverer, shield, refuge, Savior, and high tower. He saves us from violence (2 Samuel 22:2-3).

High towers, or fortified posts, were built by the Israelites in frontier or exposed places. When "every man did that which was right in his own eyes" (Judges 21:25), Gideon had a son, Abimelech, by his concubine. When Gideon died, Abimelech wanted to lead the Israelites. So he slaughtered seventy of his brothers and made himself king (Judges 9).

But God raised up some Israelites to fight Abimelech. When the evil man and his army captured the city of Thebez, the people fled to its high tower for safety. As Abimelech tried to set fire to the door of the tower, a woman dropped a millstone on his head and killed him. Those in the tower were saved.

God is better than any man-made fortress. We do not have to worry about defending ourselves, for He is our shield. If we trust Him, nothing can happen except by His permission. If He allows something to try our faith, we can rest assured that He knows it is what we need to become stronger.

Our joy is this: anytime we need a fortress, we can run to our Lord.

71

Joy in Christ's Return

BIBLE READING: 1 Thessalonians 4:13-18

A crown of righteousness . . . unto all them also
that love his appearing (2 Timothy 4:8).

When our Lord Jesus was caught up into heaven forty
days after His bodily resurrection from the grave, two angels
appeared to His amazed disciples. They said, "Men of Gali-
lee. . . . This same Jesus . . . will come back in the same
way you have seen him go into heaven" (Acts 1:11, NIV).

For almost two thousand years, Christians familiar with
this promise have awaited Christ's second coming. But many
have not been taught He is coming back. Some scoff,
"Where is the promise of his coming?" (2 Peter 3:4).
Jesus warned that He would come back unexpectedly (Matthew 24:44), and that we had better live as if He were
coming anytime, which He may (Luke 12:42-48).

How can we have joy in Christ's return unless we are living godly lives in expectation of His coming? I remember
when I was young in the Lord and was doing something
questionable. Something reminded me that Christ might
come anytime. I did not want Him to come and find me
doing that! Expecting Christ's return is one of the most
purifying influences in our lives.

The thought of Christ's soon return is a comfort and joy.
He will catch us up into the clouds with Himself and Christians who have gone before. We shall receive new, incorruptible bodies like His, and there shall be no more sorrow
or crying. Rejoice in that, and look for our Savior's soon
return.

72

Joy in God's Kindness

BIBLE READING: James 5:8-11

Like as a father pitieth his children, so the LORD
pitieth them that fear him (Psalm 103:13).

Have you ever thought about how kind God is? The
Bible says, "But when the kindness and love of God our
Savior appeared, he saved us, not because of righteous things
we had done, but because of his mercy" (Titus 3:4-5, NIV).

In this passage, the Greek word for "kindness," *chrestotes,*
carries the meaning of gentleness and comes from a root
word that means "gracious." The Greek word for "love"
here is *philanthropia.* Does that word ring a bell in your
mind? Certainly, we get our word *philanthropy* from it,
and that carries the meaning of the original Greek, which is
love for man or goodwill toward all men.

That is the way God feels toward us, in spite of all our
unloveliness! Just before Paul wrote the above verse to
Titus, he said, "At one time we too were foolish, disobedient,
deceived and enslaved by all kinds of passions and pleasures.
We lived in malice and envy, being hated and hating one
another" (3:3, NIV). If we are honest, that is exactly how
we have been at times, especially before we became Christians, and occasionally since then.

Another translation of *philanthropia* is "pity." God felt
sorry for us, the slaves of our sinful human natures, and ex-
tended His love to us.

We can experience God's joy by meditating on His kindness and by feeling kind and understanding toward others,
and praying for and helping them grow as Christians.

73

Joy in God's Presence

BIBLE READING: Psalm 73:23-28

And Enoch walked with God (Genesis 5:22).

The psalmist said, "It is good for me to draw near to God" (73:28), and so it is. What a pity so many of us miss out on the joy of His presence! So many find it difficult to even squeeze in a few minutes a day with their Lord.

Remember when you were a teenager and thought you were in love? I do. For several years I thought a trumpet player named Gene was special. I loved to be with him—talking, playing the piano and trumpet together, or going out.

If we truly love our Lord, will we not look forward to spending time with Him—talking to Him, and quietly waiting on Him to speak to us? He dearly loves us and desires our companionship. "The beloved of the LORD shall dwell in safety by him; and the LORD shall cover him all the day long, and he shall dwell between his shoulders" (Deuteronomy 33:12).

How can we hear our Beloved's blessed voice if we never stop to listen? Has He not promised to lead, teach, and guide us? This He does by His Spirit and His Word, and one is never contrary to the other.

Sometimes when I am praying and fellowshiping with God, I receive the distinct impression that He wants me to do something in relation to my prayers. I am no longer surprised when what He leads me to do results in answers to those prayers, for doesn't my Lord know everything? He helps me find things, guides me, and gives me wisdom. What joy there is in His presence!

74

Joy in God's Promises

BIBLE READING: Psalm 34:9-22

There hath not failed one word of all his good
promise (1 Kings 8:56).

How many precious promises God has given us! He
promises salvation for all who thirst for it (Revelation 22:
17) and call upon Him (Romans 10:13). He promises
forgiveness for all who repent of their sins (1 John 1:9).

He promises to supply all the needs of those who are His
children by faith in Christ (Philippians 4:19). He promises
we shall never want for any good thing (Psalm 34:10);
that His eyes are always upon us and His ears are always
open to our cry (v. 15); that He will deliver us out of all
our troubles (vv. 17-19); and that we who trust in Him
shall not be condemned (v. 22).

God promises that if we delight ourselves in Him, He will
give us the desires of our hearts (Psalm 37:4); and if we
commit our way to Him, He will take care of all the details
(v. 5). If we acknowledge Him in all our ways, He will direct our paths (Proverbs 3:6). If we honor Him with the
firstfruits of all our income, He will pour out temporal blessings for us (Proverbs 3:9-10).

God promises His children comfort (John 16:22); wisdom when we ask for it (James 1:5); peace (John 14:27);
and answered prayers and joy (John 16:24). He promises
rest to the heavy laden who come to Him (Matthew 11:28-
30), and eternal rewards to those who live for Him (Matthew 10:42). When we receive those rewards, we will enter
into the joy of the Lord (Matthew 25:23), of which we can
have a daily foretaste now if we will claim His promises and
rejoice in them!

75

Joy in God's Long-suffering

BIBLE READING: Psalm 86:4-15

Thou, O Lord, art a God full of compassion, and gracious, longsuffering (v. 15).

Have you ever offended someone and found that he or she would not forgive you, no matter how sorry you were? I had that happen to me some years ago; it gave me an awful feeling. How deeply it grieved me that the person would not forgive me when I asked forgiveness.

How wonderful that God is not like that! When I went to Him about my mistake, I found the blessed assurance of His forgiveness and understanding. He showed me that He had allowed that situation in order to teach, chastise, and humble me, so that "afterward it yieldeth the peaceable fruit of righteousness" (Hebrews 12:11).

Let's face it: we all make mistakes. I have learned through God's patience with me to be patient and understanding toward others. I have stopped looking for the perfect church, the perfect pastor, the perfect Christians. There are no such things! "All have sinned" (Romans 3: 23).

As we recognize our own fallibility and God's long-suffering toward us, we tend to have more sympathy with others' shortcomings; then we pray for them rather than criticize or judge. But God is perfect; He has never done wrong. This makes His merciful, loving patience with us even more marvelous!

It is no accident that David in thinking about God's long-suffering and compassion, sang, "Rejoice the soul of thy servant: for unto thee, O Lord, do I lift up my soul" (Psalm 86:4).

76

Joy in Praising the Lord

BIBLE READING: Psalm 150

Sing praises unto his name; for it is pleasant
(Psalm 135:3).

Do you want an instant lift into joy? Start praising the
Lord. Just look up and smile and say, "Hallelujah! Praise
the Lord! You're the greatest, Father!" and other words like
that. Fall on your knees and praise Him. Stand up and lift
your arms to heaven and praise Him. Sing praises to Him.

You do not feel like it. It was rough getting the children
off to school. You spat with your husband. The coffee
boiled over. Your neighbor told you to keep your children
off her yard. Your migraine headache is acting up. And the
cat is expecting kittens again. That is just when you need
to praise the Lord!

Praise Him that your children have a school to go to,
that you have a husband, that you have coffee to boil over.
Praise Him that you have an opportunity to show your
neighbor love in answer to hostility. Praise Him that it is
just a migraine and not a fatal illness. Praise Him that your
children have a pet.

As you start praising the Lord for the very things that
have gotten under your skin, a surprising thing will happen.
You will find your irritation and depression wiped out by
joy. For praising the Lord is a two-way street. He loves to
have you praise Him, because it shows you really love Him.
And you benefit from the spirit of praise, because it will
change your whole outlook on life. You will begin to realize
while you are praising the Lord that He can turn practically
anything into something to be thankful for.

77

Joy for Seekers

BIBLE READING: Matthew 7:7-14

Let all those that seek thee rejoice and be glad in
thee (Psalm 40:16).

Why did David, who wrote most of the psalms, know so
much about rejoicing and joy in the Lord? Perhaps a key
is in Psalm 42:1: "As the hart panteth after the water
brooks, so panteth my soul after thee, O God."

Although David was obviously very close to the Lord
through much of his life, he still hungered to be even closer.
He continually sought the Lord. And there is joy for such
seekers.

Matthew 6:33 says, "But seek ye first the kingdom of God,
and his righteousness; and all these things shall be added
unto you." What things? If we look at the context, we con-
cur they must be all that we need for survival in this life:
food, clothing, shelter. The Lord promises to provide everything we need if we will seek His righteousness and His
Kingdom.

If that is the way we live, we have nothing to worry about.
Certainly the Lord can take care of us better than we can
take care of ourselves. He always keeps His promises. So if
we have nothing to worry about, that leaves us carefree,
right? If we are carefree, then our hearts can be filled with
the joy of the Lord instead of all those fretting anxieties of
the world!

As we seek the Lord, He becomes increasingly dear to us.
The allurements of the world, with their false, temporary
pleasure, lose their grip. We rejoice in the Lord daily and
become a blessing to others.

78

Joy in Sorrow

BIBLE READING: 2 Corinthians 6:1-10

As sorrowful, yet alway rejoicing (v. 10).

Some women can conceive children readily; Hannah, Rachel, and I could not! Twelve years after the birth of my first child I was still praying that the Lord would give me another child.

While my husband was pastoring his first church, I finally became pregnant. How happy I was! Then one day I helped carry some boxes of Bible school material down to a darkened basement. Unaware that there was one more step, because of the large box I carried, I reached out my foot—into thin air! I tumbled down and hit the floor with a hard thud. That night I began to have a foreboding problem with my pregnancy.

How hard I prayed that God would help me keep that baby! After waiting so long, I thought I would just about die if I lost it. But I lost the baby.

I was alone when it happened. I crawled back into bed, turned my face to the wall, and cried wordlessly to my Lord. All at once a great serenity filled my heart; and unbelievably, I had a certain kind of joy! I was almost thankful for the tragedy that had allowed me to have this experience with God. I was able to be a testimony to my doctor, who was amazed at my serenity.

God is so good! Some time later He gave me Lori. So although life's unpredictable events may sometimes rob us of something we desire very much, if we just keep trusting the Lord and rejoicing in Him, He will make it up to us.

79

How to Have Full Joy: Fellowship

BIBLE READING: 1 John 1:1-9

And these things write we unto you, that your joy
may be full (v. 4).

What things did the apostle John tell Christians that their
"joy may be full"? In the next nine devotions we shall look
at some of his advice.

John said that if we walk in darkness, we do not have
fellowship with God. "But if we walk in the light, as he is
in the light, we have fellowship one with another" (v. 7).
If a person does not enjoy the fellowship of other Christians
enough to be eager to congregate and worship with them,
then he is not walking in the light and cannot have full joy.

Part of the joy we Christians can experience comes from
fellowshiping with those of like faith. We rejoice together
in answered prayer and in songs of praise and in testimony.
The Christian who does not attend his church's prayer meeting is missing much joy!

If we walk in the light, "the blood of Jesus Christ his Son
cleanseth us from all sin" (v. 7). Is that not a great cause
for joy?

Any sin can rob us of fellowship with God and His joy.
So God has made a provision for us: "If we confess our sins,
he is faithful and just to forgive us our sins" (v. 9). We
often slip up and say or do something wrong. When we do,
we must run to our Father and ask forgiveness. That way we
keep things right between us, continue to walk in the light,
and have fellowship with God and Christians—and have
full joy.

80

How to Have Full Joy: Abide in Christ

BIBLE READING: 1 John 2:28—3:3

And now, little children, abide in him (v. 28).

Abiding in Jesus brings us full joy. How do we abide in Him? First, we have to be born again through faith in Christ; then we will do what is right (2:29), for God gives us a new nature that desires righteousness and is uncomfortable with sin. The Holy Spirit is conforming us to our Lord's image (Romans 8:29).

As God's children, we are objects of His love (1 John 3:1). The divine Husbandman has grafted us into the vine (John 15:1-2), and Jesus wants us to abide in Him so we may bear fruit. One way to bear fruit is to help others come to know Christ as Savior. Another is to show forth the fruit of the Spirit in our lives (Galatians 5:22-23) so they may see Christ in us and be inspired to know Him and live for Him. Joy is one fruit of the Spirit.

So we begin to look like Christ in this life if we are filled with the Spirit. When He appears, we shall be like Him (1 John 3:2). John says that everyone who has this hope purifies himself, even as He is pure (3:3).

If a friend invites you to eat and hands you a dirty dish to fill with food, you would want it cleaned up first! We Christians have a lot of dirty remnants of our "old man" clinging to our hearts. We need to pray and clean them out and purify ourselves. Let us open our hearts to the Holy Spirit so He can fill us and we can live righteous lives. When we are filled with the Spirit, we are abiding in Christ and have full joy.

81

How to Have Full Joy: Love One Another

BIBLE READING: 1 John 3:10-18

Whosoever doeth not righteousness is not of God,
neither he that loveth not his brother (v. 10).

Another sign John gives of a child of God is that she
loves fellow Christians. Children of the devil do not love
children of God, and the cross divides all the world into
those two categories. That is why the world hates Christians.
So do not be surprised if everyone does not love you if you
are a Christian. Remember, many hated Jesus! Even religious leaders, who should have loved God, hated and persecuted Jesus.

John mentions Cain, who in a jealous rage killed his
brother. He says Cain belonged to the evil one. Cain de-
spised Abel because his own actions were evil and Abel's
were righteous. John says anyone who hates his brother is a
murderer.

John says again and again that Christians should love one
another. "Whoever does not love does not know God, because God is love" (1 John 4:8, NIV).

A Christian friend of mine goes weekly to a rest home to
minister to lonely saints. That is love. Another helps the
less fortunate, many of whom are Christians. That is love.
Still another overlooks insults, slights, and disagreements to
keep harmony in her church. That is love.

What joy it is to help others out of a heart of love! What
joy buoys our hearts when we refuse to allow petty pouts to
mar our fellowship. What joy it is to have God's love in our
hearts. That is full joy!

82

How to Have Full Joy: Obedience

BIBLE READING: 1 John 2:1-6

If a man love me, he will keep my words (John 14:23).

According to John, when we Christians do something wrong, Jesus goes to bat for us. Perhaps he says, "Father, I know she sinned, but I died for her sins. She has repented and accepted My sacrifice for her sins. Now she is Your child, and she is sorry she fell again. Forgive her for My sake."

When we really know Jesus and realize how tenderly He cares for us, we will strive to keep His commandments: "Thou shalt love the Lord thy God with all thy heart, and with all thy soul, and with all thy strength, and with all thy mind; and thy neighbour as thyself" (Luke 10:27).

If we keep those two commandments, we will automatically keep the Ten Commandments. We will have no other gods, bow down before no graven images, not take our Lord's name in vain, and observe one day in seven unto the Lord. We will not steal, bear false witness, commit adultery, or covet. And we will respect and honor our parents. Romans 13:10 (NIV) says, "Love does no harm to its neighbor. Therefore love is the fulfillment of the law."

If we love the Lord, we will read or hear His Word so we can know how He wants us to live. We will obey Him by instruction of His Word and the leading of His Spirit. If we do not obey, we grieve the Spirit and our joy takes wings, leaving us depressed, disgruntled, and discouraged.

So John writes, "Whoever claims to live in him must walk as Jesus did" (1 John 2:6, NIV). If we walk as Jesus did, we will have full joy.

83

How to Have Full Joy: Victory

BIBLE READING: 1 John 5:1-5

But thanks be to God, which giveth us the victory through our Lord Jesus Christ (1 Corinthians 15:57).

Have you ever asked someone, "How are you doing?" and had her answer, "All right, I guess, under the circumstances"?

Under the circumstances? That is not where God wants His children to be! Through Christ's sacrifice for our sins and through the power of the Holy Spirit, God has provided the means for Christians to live victorious lives.

When we are *under* the circumstances, *they* control us. We cannot expect to have victory over the besetting sins and problems in our lives until we rise *above* the circumstances with Christ's help.

Suppose you are a slave to cigarettes, alcohol, overeating, or some other bad habit. *Under* the circumstances you can think of lots of excuses why you cannot give up that harmful pleasure. So if you try, the first time you are tempted to indulge, out trots a reasonable excuse — and you have lost again!

My friend felt convicted about smoking after she was saved. "Here, Lord, take it," she finally said. "I don't want to be enslaved to anything or anybody but You." She suffered terrible withdrawal symptoms the next week, but with God's help she came through with flying colors. She never smoked again, and she became a shining light for Jesus. She was full of joy!

Every child of God can have joy in victory, if she really wants it.

84

How to Have Full Joy: Love Not the World

BIBLE READING: 1 John 2:15-17

Do not love the world, nor the things in the world. If any one loves the world, the love of the Father is not in him (v. 15, NASB).

To love not the world is another principle given in John's first epistle that will help us to have full joy. The world and its attractions draw our hearts from our Father. The more we love this world that inflames our lower instincts, the less we will love our Savior. The more we love Him, the less we will love the world; and the more real joy we will have.

We Christians live in this world, but we are not of it. We are strangers and pilgrims in it (Hebrews 11:13). We seek a better country, a heavenly land. God has prepared a city for us (11:16). He does not want us to be attached to this world, for it has been corrupted by sin (Romans 8:21).

God tells us, "Set your minds on things above, not on earthly things. For you died, and your life is now hidden with Christ in God. . . . Put to death, therefore, whatever belongs to your earthly nature" (Colossians 3:2-5, NIV). By dying to self and this world we begin to live the abundant life.

The Lord does not want us to become oddballs; if we do, I doubt if we could reach others with the gospel. We can look attractive, and we can participate in worthwhile activities.

But the Lord and His Kingdom should always be first in our hearts. If we put Him first, everything else will fall into place—and we will have full joy.

85

How to Have Full Joy: Try the Spirits

BIBLE READING: 1 John 4:1-6

> Test the spirits to see whether they are from God
> (v. 1, NIV).

If we start following a false religion, we lose the joy of the Lord. John warns us to test the spirits.

How can we recognize the true from the false? "Every spirit that acknowledges that Jesus Christ has come in the flesh is from God, but every spirit that does not acknowledge Jesus is not from God" (1 John 4:2-3, NIV). Thus the test of a religious teacher or group is: What do they believe about Christ? Do they believe He came in the flesh? Do they believe He was both God and man, as His name indicates? Do they believe what the Bible teaches about Christ: that He was born of a virgin (Isaiah 7:14); that He died on the cross for our sins (Isaiah 53); and that He arose from the grave for our justification (1 Corinthians 15: 4-8)?

John says of those who do not believe those central doctrines of God's Word: "This is the spirit of the antichrist" (1 John 4:3, NIV). A false religion usually depends on works for salvation. Under such a system one would constantly be in doubt as to his salvation, for it depends on him and his fallible nature rather than on God and His infallible grace. It is impossible to have full joy under such a condition.

But God wants us to have the joy of assurance. John says, "If anyone acknowledges that Jesus is the Son of God, God lives in him and he in God" (1 John 4:15, NIV). God's love and reliability fill us with joy!

86

How to Have Full Joy: Assurance

BIBLE READING: 1 John 5:11-13

But as many as received him, to them gave he
power to become the sons of God, even to them
that believe on his name (John 1:12).

I attended Bible institute with my best friend, Bea. At
the beginning of a new term Anne started going with us.
As we drove home the first night, Bea said, "Anne has a
problem, and maybe you can help her, Muriel."

"What's the problem, Anne?" I asked.

"Well, I'm not sure I'm really a Christian," she answered.
"I made a decision for Christ, but I seem to be lacking something that you and Bea have."

"Would you like to make sure you belong to the Lord?" I
asked. Since Anne wanted to, we talked privately when we
got to Bea's house.

"You can't have the joy of salvation unless you know you
belong to the Lord," I said. "Are you sorry for your sins and
do you believe Jesus died for you?"

When Anne said yes, I showed her 1 John 5:11-13 and
John 1:12. "At one time I wasn't sure I was saved," I explained, "because I couldn't point to a definite time. So I
asked the Lord to forgive my sins and come into my heart
if I had never really received Him. Then I wrote the date
in my Bible by John 1:12. Why don't you do that now?"

Anne and I knelt by the bed. With tears rolling down her
cheeks, she called on the Lord to save her. When she arose
she looked like a different person, for she had the joy of
salvation. Now she was sure she was God's child.

87

How to Have Full Joy: Answered Prayer

BIBLE READING: 1 John 5:14-21

Ask, and it shall be given you (Luke 11:9).

Confidence that God will answer our prayers gives us full joy, for it imparts faith that eases our minds and paves the way for Him to answer.

After I turned my life over to the Lord, I began praying for my relatives. First my husband and my daughter, Gay, came to Jesus. Then my father gave his heart to Christ, and my mother rededicated her life to Him. But my brother and his wife turned out to be longer-term projects!

Gene led a dance band, and his wife, Betty, was a devout member of a religious group in which the gospel was not preached. I prayed four years for them, and sometimes my faith wavered in the face of what seemed an impossibility. But on my knees I claimed God's promises and wept before Him for their salvation, and the assurance came into my heart that God was going to answer.

Not long after that, Gene and Betty started attending a gospel-preaching church; some months later they received Christ as their Savior. I cannot describe my joy when they were saved! Gene is now an ordained minister.

John writes that the Lord will answer our prayers if they are in accordance with His will (1 John 5:14-15). It is God's will for all men to be saved (1 Timothy 2:4). It is His will for us to have victory as Christians, and for us to be filled with His Spirit and thus have peace, joy, love, guidance, comfort, wisdom, and an abundant life.

88

Joy in Hope

BIBLE READING: Romans 15:4-13

Rejoicing in hope (Romans 12:12).

What a terrible thing it is to feel hopeless! Shirley told me she had felt so hopeless that she had taken a whole bottle of tranquilizers. She and her husband had separated, and he had taken their three children to live with his mother until she could find a place to live. But when she went to get the children, her mother-in-law would not let her have them.

Distraught, Shirley had tossed the tranquilizers into her mouth and washed them down with a Coke. Fortunately, a friend rushed her to a hospital.

After Shirley was out of danger, she was sent to a mental institution, where she turned to the God of her childhood. During the same time, her estranged husband believed in Christ. When Shirley was released, he took her to church, where she gave her heart to Christ. Now they are in the Lord's service.

Many who live in the world fall into despair and hopelessness, but we who know Jesus can have all kinds of hope. First, there is our hope of salvation. A "hope" is something we have to trust in or look forward to. We know Christ has saved us, and our beautiful hope is that someday we shall live eternally in incorruptible, spiritually perfect bodies like Christ's (1 John 3:2-3).

Life may not be ideal, but in heaven it will be. Jesus' second coming is called "the blessed hope" (Titus 2:13, NIV). Even though we may be suffering now, we can have joy in the hope of our future with Christ!

89

Joy in Believing

BIBLE READING: Isaiah 12

Now the God of hope fill you with all joy and
peace in believing (Romans 15:13).

We can have joy in believing by remembering that the
"God of hope" is in charge! Our Father is not the God of
despair or worry or fear.

One woman was concerned about her variety store. Sales
had been low, and she needed fifteen hundred dollars to save
the business. She tried to get a loan from many places, but
was turned down continually. So although she felt assured
when she prayed that God would meet the need, she continued to worry instead of trusting Him. On a trip to visit
her daughter, she became ill from worry.

However, when she returned, she prayed for God's guidance. He led her to the bank across the street from her store,
where she readily obtained the needed loan. All that worrying, sickness, and spoiled vacation for nothing! God had
been with her all the time, and He would have relieved her
of that burden and filled her with the joy and peace of believing, if only she had trusted Him fully! He has promised
to supply all our needs (Philippians 4:19).

My Bible is filled with penciled-in dates to remind me of
when I turned to God and He gave me a verse for my need.
When God gives us such assurance, we had better believe it!
He has given us His Word to speak to us, and He is able to
guide us to the very word we need. He loves us and wants
to comfort us in every trial. And, He wants us to have His
peace and joy continually.

Faith is just believing what God says He will do.

90

Joy in Obedience

BIBLE READING: Psalm 40:1-8

I delight to do thy will, O my God (v. 8).

A well-known gospel singer-evangelist told me a remarkable story. As a teenager, Jerry had developed a good act imitating popular singers, and he had wanted nothing more than to be an entertainer. While in New York City with his high school band, he and the other band members had gone to hear Vincent Lopez and his orchestra. Lopez had called for volunteer entertainers, and Jerry's friends had thrust him on stage.

As Jerry finished singing, the crowd went wild. Afterward, an agent offered him a contract with the RKO movie studios. But the offer that fulfilled Jerry's dreams only filled his heart with turmoil. What he did not know was that all of his life his dad had been praying that he would be called to preach. Now God was dealing with him about doing His will.

Back home, Jerry knew he had to turn down the contract and seek God's will. Finally, one night alone in the woods, he yielded to God's call to full-time service. Such joy flooded his heart that he raced back home and used his bed as a trampoline!

There is joy in obedience to God's will. What has the Lord been asking you to do for Him? Has it seemed to be something of which you think yourself incapable, something that would cost you a lot, or something that seems hard or impossible? If you are sure it is a burden *God* has laid on your heart—and if it is in keeping with His Word—step out in faith and do it! If you do not know what God wants you to do, just say, "Here am I, Lord, reporting for duty!"

91

Joy in Thankfulness

<small>BIBLE READING: Deuteronomy 16:9-12</small>

In everything give thanks: for this is the will of
God in Christ Jesus concerning you (1 Thessalonians 5:18).

The Israelites had a holiday season during harvesttime
called the Feast of Weeks, which they observed unto the
Lord by His command. During that time they were to rejoice in all the Lord's blessings.

They were to remember when they were in bondage in
Egypt, and how God had delivered them through the Passover. The Feast of Weeks, which occurred fifty days after
the Passover celebration became known as Pentecost.

During one Passover celebration, our Lord became the
Lamb slain for our sins (1 Peter 1:18-20). How often we
should remember how He rescued us from sin and delivered
us out of bondage worse than Egypt's and gave us new life.
That should keep us full of joy until we go to be with Him.

Then on the day of Pentecost fifty days after Christ's sacrifice, the believers awaited Christ's promise of the Holy
Spirit. Then the Holy Spirit fell. The disciples were so filled
with joy and zeal for the Lord that the crowd that gathered
thought they were drunk.

But the joyful heart that comes when we are filled with
the Spirit is one that suffers no hangover. It causes us to
bubble over with Jesus' radiance so others will come to love
Him, too. The more we thank God for His blessings, the
more we will be filled with His Spirit and unique joy.

92

More Joy in Thankfulness

BIBLE READING: Psalm 136

In everything give thanks (1 Thessalonians 5:18).

While John and Vivian Weller were in Rome, John suddenly discovered his wallet was missing. How upset they were at first over this unexpected blow! They went to the police station, but found little interest in their problem. Then Vivian prayed and asked the Lord to send someone to help them.

Several minutes later a tall man approached the police station. He turned out to be someone very important, and he seemed genuinely concerned about the loss of the wallet. "But I doubt if you'll ever get it back," he said.

The man suggested that they go to the American embassy. On the way there Vivian and John began singing the gospel chorus, "In everything give thanks, for this is the will of God in Christ Jesus concerning you." Soon their concern lifted, and they were laughing. At the embassy, they found no help, either.

Back in their room, they prayed over the situation. Twenty-five minutes later the phone rang. John's wallet had been found by a nun and had been turned in at the very police station where my friends had gone.

Often we encounter situations in which we could worry ourselves sick. But we accomplish nothing by fretting, except to make ourselves miserable! How much better it would be if we would just start praising and thanking the Lord concerning the situation and what He will do in it! Try this when you are going through a rough experience, and have joy instead of vexation.

93

Joy in Heaven

BIBLE READING: Luke 15:1-10

Joy shall be in heaven over one sinner that repenteth (Luke 15:7).

Have you ever told a fellow Christian that someone just received Christ as his Savior, and had that person give you a "Ho-hum, so what?" look? I have. But I do not understand it! What is greater than becoming God's child?

God and the angels in heaven do not take the conversion of even one sinner for granted. The Bible says there is joy in heaven when a sinner comes to God. Imagine how important something must be to elicit that reaction in heaven!

Have you ever lost something and looked all over for it? Jesus said a woman lost one silver coin from her wedding necklace. It was a terrible loss to her since other people would think she was not a good wife. And unless she found it, she would be in trouble with her husband. After much searching she found the coin, and she was so thrilled that she ran out to share the news with her neighbors. That is the kind of joy Jesus said occurs in heaven when one sinner repents, or is "found."

We, too, experience joy when we finally find something we have lost. I lost my glasses at a camping site. My daughter's friend found them by stepping on them, and they were bent out of shape. But I was glad to see those glasses!

How much more joy should we have when someone on his way to a Christless eternity repents and comes to Jesus? Begin to pray for lost persons you know, and look for opportunities to witness to them. If you see even one saved, you will glimpse the joy in heaven!

94

Joy in Weakness

BIBLE READING: 2 Corinthians 12:7-10

My grace is sufficient for thee: for my strength is
made perfect in weakness (v. 9).

I know I am going to do my best for the Lord when I
most feel the need to lean on Him. I serve as church pianist,
and sometimes even after I have practiced and practiced a
difficult piece, I still am not sure that I will not make a
mistake. Do I ever pray while at that keyboard! And what
joy fills my heart when I have finished with reasonable skill!

With red face, however, I can recall times when I felt so
sure of myself in playing the piano or in singing while playing my accordion that I forgot to lean upon God. I quickly
learned that without Him I am nothing.

Shortly after Bea was saved, she told me one day, "They
asked me to teach vacation Bible school. Muriel, I can't do
that. You know that before I was saved all I knew how to do
was lean on a bar and drink."

"Bea," I said, "let me ask you a question. Could Jesus
do it?"

"Yes, of course!"

"Well, can't He do it then through you?"

The light dawned. Bea agreed to help. Later she held
Bible clubs at home and led many children to Christ. Eventually she became a VBS superintendent as well as junior
church director. She was well known for her joy in the Lord.

Have you experienced the joy of doing things in God's
power?

95

More Joy in Weakness

BIBLE READING: John 15:1-7

I can do all things through Christ which strengtheneth me (Philippians 4:13).

Have you been in a spot where the only place you could look was up? Often hard places provide our best experiences of God's joy, if approached by faith.

One summer I flew to Ohio to speak at a national church conference. At my stopover in Charlotte, North Carolina, I ate a hot dog.

The food poisoning did not hit immediately. No, it waited until just three hours before I was due to speak the next day. Was I ever sick! Griping pains ripped through my abdomen, and I thought, *O Father, how am I ever going to stand up and address all those people feeling like this?*

But I knew that with God nothing is impossible. So I said, *Lord, I'm just going to lean hard on You and depend on You to help me. Please just lift all these symptoms when I speak, and I'll give You all the praise!*

The terrible pains and sick feeling continued until shortly before I left my room for the auditorium. Suddenly they disappeared! As I stood there before all those delegates, completely relying on God, I felt perfectly at ease; and I spoke with what I felt was the Lord's power. Afterward I autographed my books.

As I entered my room the pains hit me again! Once more I prayed that the Lord would relieve them on my flight home, so that I could witness for Him. He did. At my stopover I had the joy of leading a woman to Christ.

The symptoms came back at home, but I was too full of God's joy to care!

96

Joy in Trusting

BIBLE READING: Proverbs 3:1-10

Trust in the LORD with all thine heart (v. 5).

In Proverbs 3:1-10 God gives the recipe for a life full of joy.

"Trust in the LORD with all thine heart; and lean not unto thine own understanding" (v. 5). Often we sacrifice joy on the altar of our assessment of a situation. If we would quit trying to understand and just trust God, we would have much more peace and joy.

"In all thy ways acknowledge him, and he shall direct thy paths" (v. 6). You don't know which way to turn? Quit worrying. Anxiety will get you nothing but a headache! God knows the best way to take. He cares enough and will lead you there, if you look to Him.

"Be not wise in thine own eyes: fear the LORD, and depart from evil" (v. 7). There is no real joy if we try to order our lives apart from God and His laws. We just make a mess of things. Countless people have.

If we trust in the Lord and obey Him in everything, He promises to make us healthier (v. 8), which helps us have more joy. Many are ill because they have violated God's health rules. They have worried themselves sick; become bitter, hostile, or unforgiving; become slaves to things that are harmful to their bodies, such as alcohol, drugs, too much rich food, caffeine, or cigarettes.

We spend huge amounts of money on indulgences and doctors. If we will honor the Lord with a tithe of our incomes instead, our presses will "burst out with new wine" (vv. 9-10). That means we will have joy!

97

Joy in Worship

BIBLE READING: Psalm 66:1-4

Make a joyful noise unto God (v. 1).

Week after week, many dutiful Christians attend their churches on Sunday. Many pay their tithes, many serve the church in some way, many rear their children in the nurture and admonition of the Lord.

But as I have worshiped in various churches, I have wondered, *Where is the joy?* As a wooden-faced choir sang about rejoicing, I have reflected, *Where is the joy?* As members of the congregation sang while barely opening their mouths, I have thought, *Where is the joy?*

Where is it? It went down the drain with their first love, their first love for Christ. Going to church is a ho-hum routine. If someone cracks a smile of joy in church, everybody looks around to see who slipped on a banana peel!

Do you experience joy in worshiping God at church and home? If not, do not compare yourself to others. Look at the Old Testament saints and how they worshiped. Notice their spirit of praise and joy in the psalms.

The way to experience joy in worship is to start praising and worshiping the Lord from your heart, both at home and at church. Before a service, while the prelude is being played, bow your head reverently and talk to the Lord. Read one of the praise psalms and get yourself into a worshipful mood. Ask the Lord to give you something special in that service. He will. In fact, if you really worship the Lord, one special thing you will have is joy.

98

Joy in Soul-winning

BIBLE READING: Psalm 126

The people that walked in darkness have seen a
great light (Isaiah 9:2).

I will never forget my joy when I first helped someone
come to know Jesus as Savior! I was fairly young in the
Lord, eager to share the Good News with everyone. I did not
know the techniques of leading a person to Christ, but I
knew the gospel and what He had done for me. So that is
what I shared.

My husband and I had bought a home in a new develop-
ment. One new friend I made was Joyce, who seemed inter-
ested in what I said about the Lord.

One day Joyce came to visit. "Guess what!" she exclaimed, her eyes shining. "I did what you said I should
do! I was doing the dishes last night and thinking about
all you had said. I got to feeling so sorry about all the
wrong things I had done, and then I realized that Jesus had
died for *me,* for *my* sins. I just bowed my head and gave
my heart to Jesus!"

I went straight up to cloud nine for joy! I felt like danc-
ing all over my living room. When once you taste the joy
of helping someone else come to know Christ, you are on
your way to a lifetime career in soul-winning. I have had
the joy of helping many come to know Jesus as their Savior
since then; yet even today the joy over one newly saved person thrills me.

What a privilege we Christians have, to help the lost and
dying come into the glorious light of Christ, to pass from
death into life! We miss one of the greatest joys of the
Christian life if we do not share our faith!

99

Joy in Controlled Thinking

BIBLE READING: Philippians 4:4-8

We take captive every thought to make it obedient
to Christ (2 Corinthians 10:5, NIV).

Do you know one way in which we lose our joy in the
Lord? We allow our thought life to run amok. We dwell
on things not pleasing to the Lord.

A problem comes into our life, and we worry about it.
Maybe we pray, but our mind keeps going back to it. Anxiety grabs us by the throat, and peace flies out the window.

Someone offends us. Our minds latch onto the offense and
we chew on it as a cow chews its cud, magnifying it out of
proportion. We remember or look for other insults from
that person. Hostility wells up in our hearts, and gone is our
joy.

I am going to tread on a touchy subject, but it is a problem that may rob many women of joy. Covetous thoughts
come sometimes. Probably the worst is when we find
another woman's husband attractive and start thinking
about him. Before we know it, we may be breaking the
tenth commandment. And if we get in too deeply, maybe
the seventh commandment, at least in our thought life.

How do we control our thought life and bring every
thought into captivity to Christ? Nip temptation in the
bud. When a thought comes to mind that you know might
lead to wrong thinking, *reject it* in His name. Start praying
and praising the Lord. Take everything to Him and trust
Him for the victory. You can do that even if you have
already fallen deeply into a wrong thought pattern. As God's
child you do not have to be a slave. Why be miserable? Get
back into God's joy!

100

Count It All Joy

BIBLE READING: James 1:1-12

Consider it pure joy, my brothers, whenever you
face trials (v. 2, NIV).

You almost have to blink your eyes to make sure you
are reading James 1:2 correctly! "Joy in the face of trials?"
the natural man in us scoffs. "He's got to be kidding! How
can I have joy when the car breaks down, when my husband
gives me a bad time, when my children get into trouble?
How can I have joy when my husband loses his job, and the
bill collectors pound on our door? How can I have joy when
everything goes wrong, I'm misunderstood, or I'm incapaci-
tated by accident or illness?"

James said it is by knowing that the testing of our faith
produces patience; that, in turn, will make us strong in character, ready for anything.

Our trials are often the discipline God administers in
love. "No discipline seems pleasant at the time, but painful . . . however, it produces . . . righteousness and peace"
(Hebrews 12:11, NIV).

Do you yearn to have a victorious Christian life that reveals Christ? God in His love is bringing it about through
those trials. Do not fight Him; do not become bitter or re-
sentful. Count it all joy.

You will become a beautiful person, and your peace and
joy will be more constant. In this sin-wracked world we will
have tribulation. But if we count it all joy, the pain will be
eased.

101

Joy for Mourning

BIBLE READING: Isaiah 61:1-3

To give unto them beauty for ashes, the oil of joy
for mourning (v. 3).

I will never forget the home-going of one dear saint of
God. She had been bedridden for some time and had suffered much. Through it all she was a blessing to all of us
who knew her. It was a joy to be with her, where we felt
the presence of the Lord.

When the Lord called her home, of course it saddened the
hearts of her loved ones. But after the funeral, only joy was
written on their faces. They were rejoicing that their mother
and grandmother had been released from that decaying,
painful shell and was now enjoying Jesus' presence.

No doubt these fine Christians had shed tears in private,
but to others they showed their confidence that she was in
heaven. Thus, even in mourning, those of us who lose a
Christian loved one can find joy. Even if we mourn the ab-
sence of a beloved one who is still alive but far removed
from us, we can find joy in the fact that, in answer to our
prayers, the Lord will keep His hand on that loved one's life.

But what if we mourn the death of an unsaved loved one?
Jesus said He came to bind up the brokenhearted, to give us
beauty for ashes, the oil of joy for mourning. When we
come to an end of ourselves and there is no human reason
for comfort, there is Jesus. Reach out and touch Him, and
let the healing balm of His presence give you joy for mourning.

102

Exceeding Joy

BIBLE READING: 1 Peter 4:12-19

Now unto him that is able to keep you from fall-
ing, and to present you faultless before the presence of his glory with exceeding joy (Jude 24).

When Christ comes back to earth to catch us up into the
clouds with Himself, we shall see the One who loved us so
much that He died for us. We shall receive new, incorruptible bodies like His; we shall know exceeding joy.

The expression "exceeding joy" is used only twice in
God's Word, and both times in relation to Christ's second
coming. Peter says that those of us who have gone through
fiery trials and have been partakers of Christ's sufferings
will be glad with exceeding joy when His glory is revealed.

Most of us know little about suffering for Christ. But if
we have been shunned or reviled for witnessing for Him,
we have been partakers of His sufferings. After I spoke to a
neighbor about his soul, he took our cat off our porch while
we were at church one Sunday, and killed it. I was brokenhearted, but I found something to rejoice in when I realized why he had been killed.

A friend of mine was locked out of her house one night
with her children because her husband was furious that she
had gone to church. But someday she will have exceeding
joy in the presence of Jesus.

Someday we all shall have exceeding joy as Jesus presents
us faultless before His Father and says, "Here they are,
Father, all those I loved enough to wash clean with My
blood, and love enough now to take as My bride."

103

Relationships of Joy

BIBLE READING: 2 Corinthians 1:12-15

We are your rejoicing, even as ye also are ours
(v. 14).

I belong to a church where I can feel love emanating
from Christian to Christian, and from members to visitors.
I often think, *How much some Christians miss by watching
a religious television program instead of coming to church!*

I know some dear shut-ins cannot go to church though
they would like to. And we Christians who can get around
certainly ought to try to bring them loving fellowship. But
Christ's plan for His church is for us to assemble together
regularly (Hebrews 10:25); exhort, teach, and encourage
one another (Colossians 3:16); support and build up the
church (Acts 2:41-47); grow in grace and the knowledge
of Him (2 Peter 3:18).

Paul and Timothy, who had a warm relationship with the
Christians at Corinth—a relationship that brought joy to all
their hearts—rejoiced that in all their dealings with the
Corinthians they had acted in holiness and godly sincerity.

Isn't that the way we Christians ought to act toward one
another? Should we not set good examples for one another?
Should we not have pure motives and love one another from
sincere hearts? Should we not have such a relationship with
one another that we can rejoice in each other? Is that not a
beautiful way to live? No wonder Paul and Timothy could
rejoice!

The way to have such a relationship with your fellow
Christians is to truly love them—every one! Then you will
have joy in fellowship.

104

Make a Joyful Noise

BIBLE READING: Psalm 95

Let us make a joyful noise to the rock of our salvation (v. 1*b*).

Would it not be lovely if we all could sing like a nightingale? But most of us are lucky if we can just hold a tune. And some of us may sound something like a frog with a sore throat!

Our pastor's voice is pleasing when he preaches. But bless his heart, when he sings he has a tendency to be tone-deaf. He does make a joyful noise unto the Lord, though, which is more than many do.

I cannot understand how Christians can stand in church week after week, holding a hymnbook in front of them and hardly opening their mouths! I remember when my sister-in-law Betty came to our gospel-preaching church the first time. She had grown up in a church where there was no congregational singing. She stood there and sang out with all her heart, entranced with the idea of singing unto the Lord. But so many of us Christians have forgotten how to make a joyful noise unto the Lord. So we miss the joy of worshiping Him.

My grandmother supported herself and her three children by taking in washing and doing it on an old scrub board. Hers was a hard life. But as she rubbed the clothes, she made a joyful noise unto the Lord by singing hymns.

Would you like to have joy right now? Open up your mouth and let a joyful noise—"Amazing Grace," "O for a Thousand Tongues to Sing," or some other hymn you know—fly up to heaven.

105

Joy in Work

BIBLE READING: Proverbs 31:10-31

And thou shalt rejoice before the LORD thy God in all that thou puttest thine hands unto (Deuteronomy 12:18b).

Most of us spend our days doing some kind of work. Many women have a full-time job staying at home and taking care of the house and children, which I believe is a mother's number-one, God-given responsibility.

One of the greatest things a mother can do for God and the world is to instill godly character into her children and the desire to serve the Lord. Millions came to Christ because Susannah Wesley felt that was her calling.

A homebound woman can also inspire and encourage her husband. Many a man has come to know Christ through his wife's godly example. Many a man has become a success because of a fine woman's influence.

Proverbs 31, however, indicates that the ideal woman did not just stay at home. She had many enterprises. Not only did she feed and clothe her household, but she also was a businesswoman. She also found time to help the poor and needy.

She was full of wisdom, which means she had a close relationship with God. No doubt she served Him with the talents He had given her. Obviously she lived according to the principles found in 1 Corinthians 10:31: "Whether therefore ye eat, or drink, or whatsoever ye do, do all to the glory of God." If you live by that, you cannot help but be enthusiastic about whatever you put your hand to — and in it you will find joy.

106

Joy in Little Things

BIBLE READING: Psalm 105:1-5

O give thanks unto the LORD. . . . Remember his marvellous works (vv. 1-5).

While driving one day it occurred to me what a privilege and pleasure it was to drive a car. *If I had been born in another time,* I thought, *I would never have enjoyed this privilege of getting so quickly from one place to another!* Thinking of my sisters of bygone years, who had had to either walk or ride in a slow carriage, I was filled with joy and praised the Lord that I was privileged to be born in the twentieth century.

I walked by a field and stopped to pick a wild flower, Queen Anne's lace. Looking at the multitude of delicate flowerettes in its umbel, I noticed a tiny purple blossom near the center. This cunning creation of God's touched me so much that tears of joy sprang to my eyes. How beautiful that God should lavish such intricacy of detail on a wild flower! So I praised the Lord.

Sitting in the church choir, I looked at the congregation. I thought, *How good the Lord was to lead us to this church.* As I meditated on God's goodness, I began making melody in my heart to Him.

You know, we can have so many more thrills of joy in our lives if we would just stop and notice the little blessings we take for granted!

Right now, think of some of them. Are you happy you have a washing machine instead of a scrub board? Does your pet bring you joy? Do you appreciate your fireplace on a cold night? What do you have to be grateful for right now?

107

Joy Cometh in the Morning

BIBLE READING: Psalm 30

Weeping may endure for a night, but joy cometh
in the morning (v. 5).

How easy it is for those of us who try to stay close to the
Lord to have His joy in our hearts! But cause for weeping
comes into the lives of every one. The worst time of all is
at night. Though you may go to sleep, you awaken in the
night and your burden seems almost unbearable. Tears flow
freely.

The husband of one of my friends died suddenly, and I
spent the night with her and her four children. During the
night I was awakened by a heartrending wail. My friend's
loss had hit her in the wee hours of the morning with the
force of a sledgehammer. I found her crying her heart out.
All I could do was put my arms about her and cry with her.
When she had cried herself out, we prayed.

When the dark night was past, my friend picked up the
pieces of her life. Several years later God gave her a Christian husband; she then had the joy of having a Christian
home, which she had not had before. Though the night be
dark sometimes, joy cometh in the morning, dear one!

Yet even through the dark night of tears, the Good Shep-
herd is there comforting us. Isn't it precious that during
the darkest hours of our lives we are most conscious of His
presence? Those are the times that we come to know Him
so much more intimately, perhaps because the only relief
we can find is in throwing ourselves completely upon Him!
So when morning finally comes, we have joy because we are
closer to the Lord than ever before.

108

Joy in God's Law

BIBLE READING: Psalm 1

But his delight is in the law of the LORD (v. 2).

What is the law of the Lord in which we can delight? The psalmist referred to God's rules in that part of the Old Testament written before his day, the Law of Moses: the Ten Commandments, the statutes governing Jewish life, the ritualistic rulings, the sacrificial provisions. Although the Law was a yoke of bondage (Galatians 5:1), he delighted in it. He knew any rule from God was holy, right, and good; and following it would lead to a blessed life.

How much more should we Christians delight in God's law, for we do not live under the bondage of the Old Testament statutes; we live under grace. Jesus said, "For my yoke is easy, and my burden is light" (Matthew 11:30).

What is God's law for us Christians then? It is the royal law of love (James 2:8). We are to love the Lord with all our hearts, souls, and minds; and our neighbors as ourselves (Matthew 22:37-39). That sounds simple, but we have to do a lot of meditating to apply it! It involves being sold out to God, to the place where He is our all-in-all. It involves loving our fellowman so much that we will not do anything to hurt him or cause him to stumble.

If we live by that royal law of love, we will be the most joyful people in this world! But to live by it, we need to study God's Word for His instructions on applying it. God's Word is full of His counsel for a blessed life. What joy we can have in the wisdom God shares daily through His Word!

Joy in God's Approval

BIBLE READING: Luke 1:26-38

But he that glorieth, let him glory in the Lord. For not he that commendeth himself is approved, but whom the Lord commendeth (2 Corinthians 10: 17-18).

Consider Mary's faith in God when she said to the angel Gabriel, "Behold the handmaid of the Lord; be it unto me according to thy word" (Luke 1:38).

Gabriel had just told her that she would be impregnated by the power of the Holy Spirit. She who had not yet come together with her betrothed husband, Joseph, would be with child! According to Jewish law, Mary's and Joseph's betrothal was sacred, as if they had already been wedded. Any breach of it would be treated as adultery. What then would be the consequences if Mary were found with child? Joseph could divorce her either publicly or privately. In either case, Mary would face the shame of bearing an illegitimate child.

But God knew exactly what kind of young woman He had chosen to bear His only begotten Son, Jesus. "Hail, thou that art highly favored," the angel greeted Mary. "The Lord is with thee: blessed art thou among women" (Luke 1:28).

As Mary stared at Gabriel in awe, he said, "Fear not, Mary: for thou hast found favour with God" (Luke 1:30). Mary must surely have cared more for God's approval than for anything else, for she bowed to His will, trusting in Him to take care of the details.

Mary cried joyfully to her cousin, Elizabeth, "My soul doth magnify the Lord, and my spirit hath rejoiced in God my Saviour" (Luke 1:46-47).

110

Joy for One More Day

BIBLE READING: Isaiah 38:16-20

> My son, forget not my law; but let thine heart keep
> my commandments: for length of days, and long
> life, and peace, shall they add to thee (Proverbs
> 3:1-2).

An elderly man in a nursing home said one rainy day,
"Every day the sun is shining for me, because the Lord has
given me one more day to live." What a beautiful outlook!
This man must be a blessing to everyone around him, for
the sunshine of a thankful spirit radiates to others.

The apostle Paul said, "For to me to live is Christ, and to
die is gain . . . to depart, and to be with Christ . . . is far
better" (Philippians 1:21-23). He suffered greatly for
God: a stoning, beatings, prisons, chains, revilings, ship-
wrecks. No wonder he desired to be with Jesus! But he
conceded that it would be better for his fellow Christians
if he continued on earth a little longer.

Our human instinct is to survive. It is natural to want to
live a bit longer on earth. It can be a spiritual desire, too,
as it was with Paul, if our main reason is to continue serving our Lord in this needy world.

Each day we have here on earth is a gift from God. Do
we treasure it as such? Do we thank Him for it and seek
His will for that day? Twenty-four hours. How shall we use
them? Shall we rejoice in the Lord always, as the Bible
says—in every waking hour? Then we shall not only have
joy, but the Lord will use our lives greatly for His glory.

111

Joy in Captivity

BIBLE READING: 2 Kings 5:1-3, 9-15

To proclaim liberty to the captives (Isaiah 61:1).

The young Jewish girl heard the thudding sound of horses' hooves. She looked up startled, fear filling her breast. Then she heard loud sounds, cries, and screams. A big rough-looking Syrian burst into her home. "Ah," he exclaimed, "you will make a fine slave for our captain!"

He grabbed her and threw her over his shoulder. "Mother!" she screamed. "Father!" Her screams were unheard, for her parents also had been taken captive.

Carried away to a strange land, the homesick little maid became the slave of the great Syrian captain, Naaman. But in her captivity she clung to God.

When the girl learned that her master had leprosy, her heart went out to him. "Would God my lord were with the prophet that is in Samaria!" she told her mistress. "For he would recover him of his leprosy" (2 Kings 5:3).

After Naaman was told what the girl had said, he went to Israel to seek healing; following the prophet Elisha's directions, he found it—and God.

That maiden must have had great joy in helping a great leader come to know her God. Similarly, if you feel you are in some kind of captivity, you still can find joy doing something for God.

Captive to a bed, a prison, a cruel husband, a hostile environment? You can pray. Prayer releases God's power for others. When you comfort, encourage, and help others come to God, you will get a joyful blessing too.

112

Joy in Jerusalem

BIBLE READING: Isaiah 66:5-13

And they lived and reigned with Christ a thousand
years (Revelation 20:4).

There is coming, perhaps very soon, a day when the King
of kings will rule the world from Jerusalem (Zechariah 14:
8-9). Many Christians believe this day is near because it
appears as if the prophecy in Isaiah 66:8 has been fulfilled
in our time: a nation, Zion, was born in a day, in 1948.

After God gave this prophecy, He said, "Rejoice ye with
Jerusalem, and be glad with her, all ye that love her" (Isaiah
66:10). Why rejoice? Because the Lord "will extend
peace to her like a river" (v. 12). But the Bible says that
before that day of peace, Jerusalem will go through much
tribulation. After that Jesus will come from heaven to
judge the world and deliver Jerusalem. Then He will assume
His throne in Jerusalem. We will be in the army that fol-
lows in His train, clothed in white linen (Jude 14-15; Revelation 19:14). We will reign with Him (Luke 19:15-17;
2 Timothy 2:12).

Jerusalem's original name was Salem, which means
"peace." In Lamentations 2:15, Jerusalem is called "The
perfection of beauty, The joy of the whole earth." In Zechariah 8:3 it is called "a city of truth." For us it will be all
this and more, because our King of kings will be reigning
there.

Though in this life you may find it hard to rejoice, yet
even now you can rejoice in Jerusalem, in the life you will
have there with your Master!

113

Joy of Reward

BIBLE READING: Psalm 37:23-29

Well done, good and faithful servant, . . . enter
thou into the joy of thy lord (Matthew 25:23).

Those of us who serve the Lord faithfully will receive rewards not only in the sweet bye and bye but also in the here and now. God's promises in His Word are for all those who love Him.

Among earthly rewards that God promises the faithful are peace, joy, abundant life, provision of all their needs, help, deliverance, and a happy, long life. Some of these we may not all receive. For instance, it may please God to take us home sooner than later. But He does reward us in many ways.

My parents, who are in their seventies now, have been loving and serving the Lord faithfully since their early fifties. Their brothers and sisters and most of their contemporaries who did not know the Lord are gone. But they are a blessing to everyone they meet. The Lord has provided for all their needs, and they are enjoying a contented old age. It is a comfort and joy to them that my brother and I are in the Lord's service, and all their grandchildren know the Lord.

Eternal rewards in heaven await them, too. We have no idea what the Lord's rewards will be, but they surely will be more wonderful than anything we can imagine! So rejoice in the Lord's rewards in this life and the next.

114

Joy in New Clothing

BIBLE READING: Isaiah 61:10-11

Let thy priests be clothed with righteousness; and
let thy saints shout for joy (Psalm 132:9).

When we give our hearts to Jesus, He gives us new clothing! When we turn in the filthy rags of our own righteous-
nesses (Isaiah 64:6), Jesus clothes us with the spotlessly
white garment of salvation; He covers us with the robe of
His righteousness. Praise the Lord, we do not have to continue living in those dirty, sin-stained garments of the
world.

The apostle Peter said that we Christians are "a royal
priesthood" (1 Peter 2:9). The special garments for the
Israelite priests were to be "for glory and for beauty" (Exodus 28:2), so the priests would be reminded of their high
calling and behave themselves accordingly, and so others
would learn to have reverence for God.

Today, if we saints are clothed with the robe of Christ's
righteousness, and if we let Him wash our feet periodically
so that we walk in His steps, will not those with whom we
come in contact daily see Jesus in us and desire to know Him
too? Peter admonished us to be subject to one another and
be clothed in humility (1 Peter 5:5). True humility is the
most winsome grace, and it reflects the Spirit of Jesus with
rainbow colors. The closer we draw to Him, the more we
will be clothed with humility. For we realize more and more
that if there is anything beautiful or worthy about us, it is
all from Him.

Let us then put on the garment of praise (Isaiah 61:3)
and shout for joy!

115

Joy in God's Compassions

BIBLE READING: Lamentations 3:19-32

His compassions fail not (v. 22).

Today's text says about our Lord: "His compassions fail not. They are new every morning: great is thy faithfulness" (Lamentations 3:22-23).

Are you gloriously and gratefully aware in your life that God's compassions are new every morning? If you are, then you will be able to rejoice in the Lord every morning, no matter what problems you face, what burdens you bear, what crushing experience you have had. If you are His child, He is there every morning with new compassions for you.

"New compassions" means that in your latest trial He has some unique spiritual experience and strength to impart to you, something sweetly new. Or if all is going well, He has some new revelation from His Word to bless your heart. The Hebrew root word used for "compassions" here is *racham,* which means "to fondle," to caress tenderly and lovingly. God loves us so much that He will touch us with His Spirit that way every morning.

Perhaps you have not been aware of this ministry of God in your life. Why was Jeremiah, who wrote Lamentations, aware of it. Here is the answer: "The LORD is my portion, saith my soul; therefore will I hope in him. The LORD is good unto them that wait for him, to the soul that seeketh him" (vv. 24-25).

When the Lord is our portion, He is our all in all. We are always conscious of Him and His blessings. We wait on Him, we seek Him, and He is good to us. Every morning He pours out new compassions to fill our hearts with joy!

116

Joy in Healing

BIBLE READING: Jeremiah 33:6-11

Call unto me, and I will answer thee, and shew thee great and mighty things, which thou knowest not (Jeremiah 33:3).

I believe God heals in answer to prayer (Mark 11:24; James 5:15). The most important healing is the healing of the soul. It is found in Christ, "the Branch of righteousness" (Jeremiah 33:15). "He was wounded for our transgressions, he was bruised for our iniquities: . . . and with his stripes we are healed" (Isaiah 53:5). People today are soul-sick. They are not right with God, and they cannot stand themselves! They need Jesus.

Another healing is of the mind, which frequently occurs when a person receives Christ as Savior or gets right with the Lord (2 Timothy 1:7). One friend of mine was classified as manic-depressive when she was in a mental institution. But when she turned to the Lord, she was transformed.

I have heard many testimonies of physical healing, too. One woman prayed as she lay on the operating table awaiting an operation for cancer. She felt then that God touched her body, so she refused to have the operation. Tests revealed that the cancer had disappeared. Twenty years later, she is still going strong.

Has the Lord healed you in one of these three ways? Rejoice in Him. If you need healing, pray to Him in faith believing. Although God does not always choose to heal us physically (2 Corinthians 12:7-9), He will compensate by giving us joy in our weakness and in His strength!

117

Joy in Deliverance

BIBLE READING: Psalm 118:1-8

I called upon the LORD in distress: the LORD answered me, and set me in a large place (v. 5).

Nabal was an ill-natured fellow, "churlish and evil in his doings" (1 Samuel 25:3). He had an intelligent wife named Abigail, whom he probably knocked about and cursed. No doubt she often cried to God for help.

One day Nabal sarcastically refused to give David and his men food. They girded on their swords to teach Nabal some manners. But Abigail, upon hearing what had happened, hastily prepared food and brought it to David. Apologizing for her husband, she saved the lives of all his household.

Ten days later "the LORD smote Nabal, that he died" (1 Samuel 25:38). Abigail was delivered from her oppressor and David took her as his wife. Thus she became the wife of a king, set in a large place.

Perhaps you are in an unbearable situation. Keep looking to Jesus. "Rest in the LORD, and wait patiently for him" (Psalm 37:7). God will help you. As you rest in Him, you may have joy in the knowledge that He answers prayer.

Perhaps God has delivered you from a life of sin, enslavement to a wretched habit, an illness, or an unhappy situation. Do not miss out on the joy you can have in frequently recalling all He has done for you! Whenever you are feeling low, remember past mercies and deliverances. The joy and thanksgiving you felt then will well up in your heart again.

118

Joy in Revival

BIBLE READING: Psalm 138

Wilt thou not revive us again: that thy people may rejoice in thee? (Psalm 85:6).

A teenager just back from a Christian camp literally glowed as she gave her testimony. "I hadn't really wanted to go," she confessed, "because I was afraid the Lord might speak to me about some things in my life. He did, all right! I finally couldn't stand it any longer! I yielded my life to Christ, and now I'm the happiest I have ever been!"

What joy fills our hearts as we yield fully to the Lord! Why do we fearfully draw back? He desires to give us His best, which is far better than the earthly five-and-ten-cent baubles we cling to so tenaciously.

Early in my Christian experience I attended a church that had many stringent rules. I thank the Lord for that, for it brought me to the place where I fell on my knees and said, "All right, Lord, if You want me to give all these things up, I'll do it for You!" What joy I had!

Now here is the surprise! The Lord showed me that there were some things I should put out of my life; but on the other hand, that church had some prohibitions that did not jibe with what the Bible teaches! He had led me that way to try me, to see if I would be willing to give up everything for Him.

But God does not take all enjoyment out of our lives! Oh, no, we just start to live when we turn everything over to Him. Revival of our spiritual life comes when we do that. And joy is a by-product.

119

Joy in Sainthood

BIBLE READING: Colossians 1:9-14

Called to be saints, with all that in every place call upon the name of Jesus Christ our Lord (1 Corinthians 1:2).

Many people believe that only certain Christians can be called saints. However, the worst Christians to whom a letter in the New Testament was written were the Corinthians. Those characters quarreled among themselves, were conceited, tolerated gross immorality by one of their members, went to law against one another, had to be warned against fornication and idolatry, and needed a lecture on love. Yet the apostle Paul addressed them as "saints."

Everyone of us who is honest with herself knows she falls short of God's glory. I know I still have a long way to go to be like Jesus! Yet if we have repented and have trusted Jesus as our Savior, we are saints, as you can see in the Scripture quoted above. We have been sanctified—set apart and made holy—"through the offering of the body of Jesus Christ once for all" (Hebrews 10:10).

Paul also told the Corinthians, "God made him who had no sin to be sin for us, so that in him we might become the righteousness of God" (2 Corinthians 5:21, NIV). Isn't it great? God looks at us through the blood of His Son and sees us washed clean! Though we are no longer held accountable for our sins as far as salvation is concerned, we should certainly live a life that is well pleasing to our Father in heaven. Let us rejoice in our sainthood!

120

Filled with the Holy Spirit

BIBLE READING: Ephesians 5:18-21

And the disciples were filled with joy, and with the
Holy Ghost (Acts 13:52).

Ultimately all our joy in the Lord must come from the
Holy Spirit, for the fruit of the Spirit is joy. The first believers had that joy because they were filled with the Spirit.
Usually we have that joy when we receive Christ as Savior,
but many of us tend to slack off in our fervor and love for
Him. Apparently this was true also of the Ephesians (Revelation 2:1-4).

So when the apostle Paul wrote to the Ephesians, he reminded them to be filled with the Spirit (Ephesians 5:18).
He also counseled them not to be drunk with wine. Why
the comparison? When the Spirit first fell upon the disciples, they were so full of zeal and joy that people thought they
were drunk!

Wine makes a person feel cheerful (Psalm 104:15) and
loosens his tongue (Proverbs 23:29). But God counsels
His people to be filled with the Spirit, who gives us true
joy and loosens our tongues to speak for Christ.

How do we become filled with the Spirit? The Bible says:

I beseech you . . . by the mercies of God, that ye present your bodies a living sacrifice, holy, acceptable
unto God, which is your reasonable service. And be
not conformed to this world: but be ye transformed by
the renewing of your mind, that ye may prove what is
that good, and acceptable, and perfect, will of God
(Romans 12:1-2).

We must seek and obey His will to have continual joy.